CRAPS—BLACKJACK—ROULETTE—
BACCARAT—SLOT MACHINES—KENO

Do You Really Know How to Gamble?

The novice hopes he knows—and the expert is sure he knows. But the gambler who wants the odds in his favor will read and study this invaluable, computer-analyzed approach to casino games.

The authors skillfully explain the game of craps, noting the best bets (pass-line and don't-pass bets, come and don't-come bets, odd bets, etc.) for *you* and *not* the Casino.

In a short time you'll acquire basic blackjack strategy and go on to master complex count strategy—and the winning art of betting strategy.

GAMBLE WITH PROVEN ODDS—
NOT WITH LADY LUCK!

A Book On
Casino
Gambling

WRITTEN BY A
MATHEMATICIAN
AND
A COMPUTER
EXPERT

Virginia L. Graham, C. Ionescu Tulcea

PUBLISHED BY POCKET BOOKS NEW YORK

POCKET BOOKS, a Simon & Schuster division of
GULF & WESTERN CORPORATION
1230 Avenue of the Americas, New York, N.Y. 10020

Copyright © 1978 by Litton Educational Publishing, Inc.,
a Division of Litton Educational Publishing, Inc.

Published by arrangement with Van Nostrand Reinhold Company
Library of Congress Catalog Card Number: 78-16575

ISBN: 0-671-43515-9

First Pocket Books printing February, 1980

10   9   8   7   6   5   4

POCKET and colophon are trademarks of Simon & Schuster.

Printed in the U.S.A.

PREFACE

In this book we describe the main Casino games, Craps (Dice), Roulette, Blackjack (or 21), Baccarat, Slot machines and Keno, as played in the state of Nevada, Puerto Rico and other parts of the world.

The book is written for the general public. Its reading does not assume gambling experience or, in fact, any kind of special knowledge.

The methods of play we indicate are, of course, based on mathematical and computer analysis. However, except for a short technical appendix where several computations are gathered, we do not present any theoretical considerations here. Only the practical aspects of the games are discussed.

We believe that nobody should enter a Casino and gamble without first reading a book like this. The games we describe here have been completely analyzed, and there is no doubt whatsoever about the conclusions we present. For instance, if somebody plays Roulette long enough, we may predict with practical certainty what amount of money will change hands. This is done on the basis of the same mathematical principles which are used for organizing a state or a national lottery or for deciding what premiums we must pay for various insurance policies.

Unfortunately, with the exception of Blackjack, there are no strategies a player can use in Casino play which assure continuous winnings. However, it makes a lot of difference whether or not the games are played skillfully. The gambler who decides to play Craps may place, for example, Pass line bets, Don't pass bets, Field bets, Hardway bets, etc. The Pass line bets and the Don't pass bets are substantially more advantageous; hence, it is better to place only these bets. If the player also learns how to place Odds bets, the chance of a winning streak is greatly increased. Odds bets are often ignored in books on gambling. Here they are, described in detail.

As far as Blackjack is concerned, it is possible to devise winning strategies. Two new methods of play are described in Chapter 3. The first one is a simple method and can be easily mastered. It is mainly for the occasional weekend gambler. The second, the Complex point count, is for the player who will spend substantial time in training. Since this strategy is extremely powerful, especially for finding favorable betting situations, it should not be surprising that it takes a certain effort to play it well. After all, think how long it would take to learn, for example, how to hit a good forehand in tennis. Why should we expect that mastering a powerful winning Blackjack strategy requires less effort than learning how to play a fair game of tennis?

The gambler who does not want to spend time training may just consider the Blackjack Basic strategy. This method of play can be mastered in a couple of hours and is the best for the player who does not try to remember any of the cards already played.

We conclude these remarks on Blackjack by noticing that it was E. O. Thorp who first published Blackjack winning strategies and that our research was strongly influenced by his work.

The authors wish to express their thanks to the editorial staff of Van Nostrand Reinhold for the cooperation and assistance received in the publication of this book.

CONTENTS

Contents

Contents

A BOOK ON

CASINO GAMBLING

WRITTEN BY A
MATHEMATICIAN
AND
A COMPUTER
EXPERT

1
CRAPS

Craps is a game played with *two dice* on a table with a relatively high board and a layout as in Fig. 1.

There are small variations in the design of the layout, depending usually on the town you are in. However, these variations will not cause any problem as soon as the player becomes familiar with one type of layout.

The game is conducted by four Casino employees, the Boxman, the Stickman (or Croupier) and two dealers. They are positioned around the table as shown in Fig. 1. The main responsibility of the Boxman is to supervise the game. The main duties of the Stickman and Dealers will become clear during the description of the game.

To place bets at a Craps table (what type of bets can be placed will be indicated further below) the player needs chips, which can be bought at the table (or in some places, at the cashier's cage). To buy chips at the table, the player places money in front of one of the dealers. The dealer gives the money to the Boxman who counts the amount and drops it into the money box. Then the dealer places an equivalent amount in chips in front of the player. The chips should not

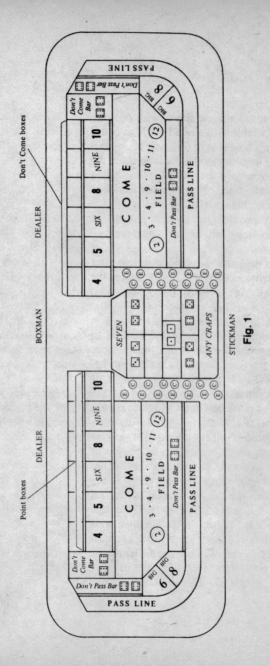

Fig. 1

be left on the table, since they may be mistaken for bets. They should be placed in the grooves provided on the border of the table.

The house establishes a *minimum* and a *maximum* bet for each table, and the corresponding amounts are usually prominently indicated. The number of players at a Craps table is limited only by the space available.

DICE AND OUTCOMES

Everybody knows what a *die* is, that it has six faces and that each face is marked with from one to six dots. We identify the faces of the die by one of the numbers 1, 2, . . . , 6. For instance, 4 will *identify the face marked by four dots*.

Assume that the die is *rolled (thrown)* on the table. If after the roll the *upper face* of the die (parallel with the surface of the table) is for example 3, we say that the *outcome* is 3, or that we have *rolled* (or *thrown*) 3.

When we roll an *honest* die on the table, we have no reason to expect that the outcome will be, for instance, 5 instead of 2. The chance of each one of the *outcomes* 1, 2, . . . , 6 is the same.*

If we *throw two dice*, 36 different outcomes are possible. We understand this easily if we assume (if the reader finds it necessary) that one of the dice is white and the other is red. At a Craps table, both dice have the same color. If, for

---

*If a *coin* is tossed a large number of times, each one of the two sides (*head* or *tail*) will turn up about the same number of times. For this reason we say that the *probability* of the *outcome head* and that of the *outcome tail* are equal to ½. Each one of the outcomes head and tail will be produced *on the average* once in every *two* tosses.

If a *die* is rolled a large number of times, then for each face S ($S = 1, 2, . . . , 6$) the quotient

$$\frac{\text{number of times the outcome was } S}{\text{number of rolls}}$$

is about 1/6. The more times we roll the die, the better the chance that the above quotient is close to 1/6. For this reason we say that the *probability* of the outcome S is 1/6. Each one of the outcomes 1, 2, . . . , 6 will be produced *on the average* once in every *six* throws.

example, 3 is rolled with the white die and 5 with the red one, we say that the *outcome is* (3, 5) or that we *rolled* (or *threw*) (3, 5). Since with each one of two dice we may roll any one of the faces 1, 2, 3, 4, 5, 6 and since

$$6 \times 6 = 36$$

it follows that there are 36 possible outcomes. As in the case of one die, it is quite obvious that the chance of each one of these 36 outcomes is the same.

At a Craps table we are not *directly* concerned with the numbers we roll with each one of the two dice, but *with the sum, or total, of these numbers*.

If we have thrown for example (3, 5), the corresponding sum, or total, is 8. If we have rolled (1, 6) or (6, 1) the sum, or total is 7. Of course the sum, or total, is 7 whenever we roll

$$(1, 6) \quad (6, 1) \quad (2, 5) \quad (5, 2) \quad (4, 3) \quad (3, 4).$$

Assume that we have thrown (3, 5), for example. If we are interested only in the corresponding sum, we shall often say that the *outcome is* 8, or that we have *rolled* (or *thrown*) 8.

However, to understand why certain bets are more favorable than others, it is necessary to have some idea of the relation between the outcome as a pair and the outcome as a total.

Of course, *for playing well* it is not necessary to understand why certain bets are better than others. It is *enough* just to know which ones of the bets are more favorable to the player, and this will be indicated in the sections below.

At this stage the following story, contributed by one of the two authors, might be instructive: "When I was about twelve years old, my cousin and I found several dice in our home. We picked *two* and decided to play a dice game. I do not know why, but probably I thought of 10 as being a lucky number. Whence, being older than my cousin, I decided that the game should be played as follows: we throw the dice and, if the total were 8 my cousin would win. If the total were 10, I would win. We started rolling the dice on a ping-pong table in the garden. Quickly my cousin won all the money I had in my pocket. I was certain that the *luck must turn* (?!?) and hence I insisted on continuing. My cousin continued to win as quickly as before, and soon I found myself owing him my next week's allowance. His continuous winning seemed, to both of us, so unbelievable (in fact, as we shall see below, it was quite *normal*) that after a while we decided to stop.

I forgot this experience soon afterwards. Many years later, while in college, I was studying Probability theory and reading about a problem posed to Galileo by an Italian gambler and about its solution. The problem was, why when you throw three dice is the *total* 10 rolled more often than the *total* 9.

With surprising precision I remembered then the game I had with my cousin and I understood immediately why he was winning. The answer was extremely simple and obvious: when you roll two dice *the total is* 10 only when the outcome is

$$(4, 6) \quad (5, 5) \quad (6, 4)$$

but the *total is* 8 each time the outcome is

$$(2, 6) \quad (3, 5) \quad (4, 4) \quad (5, 3) \quad (6, 2).$$

You roll 10 only in three ways, while you roll 8 in five different ways. Hence there is a greater chance to roll 8 than to roll 10. In fact the chance of rolling 8 is obviously almost twice as great as that of rolling 10. This is why my cousin won so quickly."

Yes, but what about *luck*, certain gamblers will ask? Did he wear a red hat that day? The fact is, that in the long run, *luck* cannot offset an edge against you. There is no doubt about it.

Casinos like to emphasize directly and mainly indirectly the idea that you should win if you are lucky and that, after all, it is not hard to be lucky. This of course does not make too much sense. However, most players believe that they are lucky (even when they say the contrary). Hence, here is a chance to find *new lucky patrons.*

We like to look at all those pictures advertised by the Casinos. All the gamblers look so happy and are all smiles. Since it is hard to believe that somebody will smile too much while losing, we assume that the Casinos suggest that most players are winning. How nice!

So that we may understand why some bets are better than others we give here the following table (it does not have to be remembered by the player):

2 can be rolled only in one way (namely (1, 1)).
12 can be rolled only in one way (namely (6, 6)).
3 and 11 can (each) be rolled only in two ways.
4 and 10 can (each) be rolled only in three ways.
5 and 9 can (each) be rolled only in four ways.
6 and 8 can (each) be rolled only in five ways.
7 can be rolled in *six* ways.

Hence, *when you roll two dice, the outcome having the best chance is 7. The outcomes with the least chance are 2 (snake-eyes) and 12 (box cars).*

On the average the outcome will be 7 once in every 6 rolls. The outcome will be 2 once in every 36 rolls. The outcome will be 3 once in every 18 rolls. The outcome will be 12 once in every 36 rolls.

COME-OUT ROLLS AND POINT ROLLS

The dice at a Craps table are thrown by one of the players participating in the game. To understand the rules of the game you should know when a throw of the dice is a *Come-out roll* and when it is a *Point roll* (these are the only types of rolls encountered at a Craps table).

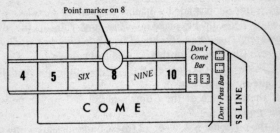

Fig. 2

Assume for instance that Sandi arrives at a table where a player gets ready to throw the two dice. Will the roll be a Come-out or a Point roll? Sandi may learn immediately of what type the roll is, by looking at the two *large discs, usually white* (the *Point markers*) on the table. If they *are placed clear of Point boxes,* the roll is a *Come-out* (when the Point markers are clear of Point boxes, they are usually placed either close to the chips box or in the *Don't come* areas). If the discs *are placed in Point boxes (in fact they are not placed completely inside Point boxes, but are positioned as in* Fig. 2) the roll is a *Point roll*. It is enough to determine only where one of the discs is, since either *both* are clear of the Point boxes or *both* are in Point boxes (*with the same number*). The Stickman will often shout "*Coming out,*" before a Come-out roll.

The first roll made by a player arriving at a table where previously there were no players is a Come-out roll. Also every roll, following a throw the outcome of which is 7, is a Come-out. Other cases when a roll is a Come-out roll are mentioned further below. In any case the position of the

Point markers will always tell the arriving player whether the next roll is a Come-out or a Point roll.

PASS LINE BETS

A *Pass line bet* is made by placing chips in the *Pass line area*. Such a bet can be placed before any roll of the dice. However, *Pass line bets should be made only before Come-out rolls* (the reason for this is explained below).

Assume that John made a Pass line bet immediately before a Come-out roll. *Then*:

If the outcome of the Come-out roll is 7 or 11, he wins *even money*.

If the outcome is 2, 3, or 12 (these outcomes are known as *Craps*), John loses his bet.

In both of these cases, the next roll is also a Come-out roll.

If the outcome is any other number, that is, 4, 5, 6, 8, 9, or 10, then this number becomes *the Point*. In this case the dealer moves the Point markers to the corresponding Point boxes. For instance, if the outcome of the Come-out roll is 5, the Point markers are placed in the Point boxes marked by the number 5. John's Pass line bet is not (directly) affected. The dice continue to be rolled (these rolls are *Point rolls*) until the outcome is *either* 7 *or the Point*. If 7 is rolled *before* the Point, then John loses his Pass line bet. If the Point is rolled *before* 7, then John wins *even money*.

Once the outcome is either 7 or the Point, the *next* roll is again a Come-out roll. The payoff, when the player wins with a Pass line bet, is made by the dealer by placing an equal amount in chips next to the initial bet. *Once a Point is established on the Come-out roll a Pass line bet cannot be removed until either 7 or the Point is thrown* (the reason for this is explained below).

As we have indicated on page 6, 7 can be rolled in six ways and 11 in two ways. Hence there are eight ways in which we can get for outcome either 7 or 11. Hence, on the average, eight times in 36 throws (or once in 4.5 throws) the outcome is 7 or 11. Similarly, 2, 3 or 12 can be rolled in four ways, so that, on the average, the player wins eight times in 36 rolls and loses only four times in 36 rolls. Hence on the Come-out roll the player who makes a Pass line bet has an edge over the House. However, once a Point is established it is the House that has the advantage, since 7 will be rolled more often than any other number. And this edge is so substantial that it cancels completely the player's edge on the Come-out roll and *gives the Casino an overall advantage of about* 1.4%, *as far as the Pass line bets are concerned.* *

This means that the House gains about 1.4/100 (that is 1.4 cents or about a cent-and-a-half) of every dollar placed in the Pass line area. Hence, the player who makes one hundred, $1 Pass line bets, on Come-out rolls, loses about $1.40.

Hence we may say, summing up the above remarks, that the player has the advantage on Come-out rolls and the House on Point rolls. This is why the player should not place Pass line bets on Point rolls, and this is why the House does not allow the player to remove Pass line bets on Point rolls.

COME BETS

A player may place a Pass line bet any time during the game. However, as we have explained in the previous section, such a bet should not be placed before Point rolls, since in such a situation the House edge is too high.

If the next roll is a *Point roll*, and if a player wants to enter the game right away and make a bet similar to the Pass line bet, that player should place a Come bet. Such a bet is made by placing chips on the table, in the Come area. If you place a Come bet before a Come-out roll, your bet will be moved (usually) in the Pass line area.

---

*More precisely it is about 1.414141414%.

Assume that Carol made a Come bet. Then:

If the outcome of the next roll is 7 or 11, she wins *even money*.
If the outcome is 2, 3, or 12, Carol loses her bet.

If the outcome is any one of the remaining numbers, say 6, then 6 becomes *the Point for Carol's Come bet*. In this case the dealer moves her bet to the Point box marked by the number 6 (see Fig. 3). The bet remains there until *either 7 or 6 is rolled*. If 7 is rolled *first*, Carol loses her Come bet. If 6 is rolled *first*, Carol wins *even money*.

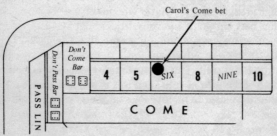

Fig. 3

We notice that the Point for Carol's Come bet may be different from the Point established by the Come-out roll.
If the bet is still in the Come area, a win is paid by the dealer, by placing an equal amount in chips, next to the player's bet. If the bet was moved to a Point box, then the dealer places first an equal amount in chips, next to the bet, and then he moves the total amount to the initial position of the bet, in the Come area.
To sum up the above discussion, we may say that a Come bet wins and loses the same way as a Pass line bet. The House edge in the case of Come bets is the same as in the case of Pass line bets, that is, about 1.4%.

Once a Come bet is placed and a Point is established, the bet cannot be removed until either 7 or the Point is rolled. The reasons for this rule are the same as in the case of Pass line bets.

DON'T PASS BETS

A *Don't pass bet* is made by placing chips in the *Don't pass area*. Such bets can be placed *only before Come-out rolls* (the reason for this will be seen below).

Assume that Carol made a Don't pass bet, immediately before a Come-out roll. Then:

If the outcome of the roll is 7 or 11, Carol loses her bet.

If the outcome is 2 or 3, Carol wins *even money*.

If the outcome is 12, she ties. Hence she neither wins, nor loses.

If the outcome is any other number, then this number becomes *the Point*. The dealer moves the Point markers to the corresponding Point boxes. The dice continue to be rolled until *either 7 or the Point is thrown*. If 7 is rolled *first*, Carol wins even money. If the Point is rolled *first*, Carol loses her bet. The payoff for a win is made as in the case of a Pass line bet.

As far as the Don't pass bets are concerned, the House has the edge on the Come-out roll. However, since the outcome having the best chance is 7, the advantage reverts to the player as soon as a Point is established.

This is why Don't pass bets are not allowed before Point rolls. The player may remove a Don't pass bet before a Point roll, but of course this should not be done.

It is often said that the Don't pass bet is the opposite of the Pass line bet. This is not quite so, since the player does not win when a 12 is thrown on the Come-out roll; he or she only *ties*. This is enough to give the *House an overall advantage of about* 1.4%. In fact, the player who makes Don't pass bets is somewhat better off than the one who makes Pass line bets, but the difference is very, very small.

Instead of tying with an outcome of 12 on the Come-out roll, in some Casinos the player will tie with an outcome of 2. Since both 2 and 12 can be produced *only in one way*, this does not change the percentage concerning Don't pass bets. However the House take increases substantially if the tie takes place with an outcome of 3 (since 3 can be produced in two ways, namely (1, 2) and (2, 1)).

When the player ties with an outcome of 12 the Don't pass area is marked (in addition to the words Don't pass) with

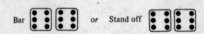

If the tie takes place with an outcome of 2 the Don't pass area is marked with

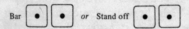

In gambling jargon, a player who places a Don't pass bet is called a *Don't bettor* or a *Wrong bettor*. In view of the above discussion we may say that if the Don't pass bettor is *wrong*, then certainly the Pass line bettor is *worse*.

DON'T COME BETS

The relation between Don't come bets and Don't pass bets is similar to that between Come bets and Pass line bets. As we have seen above, a Don't pass bet can be placed only *before* Come-out rolls. If the next roll is a Point roll, and if a player wants to enter the game right away, and make a bet similar to the Don't pass bet, that player should place a *Don't come bet*. Such a bet is made by placing chips on the table in the Don't come area.

Assume that John made a Don't come bet. Then:

If the outcome of the next roll is 7 or 11, John loses the Don't come bet.

If the outcome of the next roll is 2 or 3, he *wins even money*.

If the outcome of the next roll is 12, John ties.

If the outcome of the next roll is any other number, say 5, then 5 becomes *the Point for John's Don't come bet*. In this case the dealer moves his bet to one of the Don't come boxes marked by 5 (see Fig. 4).* The bet remains there until *either* 7

Fig. 4

or 5 is rolled. If 7 is rolled *before* 5, John wins even money. If 5 is rolled *before* 7, John loses his bet.

A win is paid in the same way as Come bets are paid. The House edge in the case of Don't come bets is the same as in the case of Don't pass bets, that is, about 1.4%.

The rules of the Casino you play in might be so that you tie when the outcome is 2 or 3 instead of 12.

---

*Although there are no numbers on the Don't come boxes, we shall often say that, for instance, the boxes behind the Point boxes marked by 5 are the *Don't come boxes marked by 5* (see Fig. 1.).

ODD BETS AND PASS LINE BETS
(TAKING THE ODDS)

A player who makes a Pass line bet is allowed to place an additional bet (associated with the Pass line bet) called an *Odds bet*, as soon as a Point has been established on the Come-out roll. The Odds bet associated with a Pass line bet is made by placing the chips as indicated in the figure below.

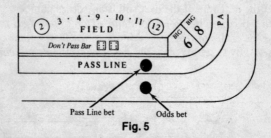

Pass Line bet   Odds bet

Fig. 5

Assume that John made a Pass line bet before a Come-out roll and that the outcome of the roll is 4. Hence the *Point* 4 is established. John may now place an Odds bet. The dice continue to be thrown until the outcome is *either* 7 *or* 4. If 7 is rolled *before* 4, the player loses both the Pass line bet and the Odds bet. If 4 is rolled *before* 7, the player wins. However, while the Pass line bet is paid even money, the way the Odds bet is paid depends on the Point. When the Point is 4, as above, the bet is paid 2 to 1.

The general rules concerning the *payoff on Odds bets*, associated with Pass line bets, are as follows:

When the Point is 4 or 10, the bet is paid 2 to 1. This means that an Odds bet of $10 wins $20.

When the Point is 5 or 9, the bet is paid 3 to 2. This means that an Odds bet of $10 wins $15.

When the Point is 6 or 8, the bet is paid 6 to 5. This means that an Odds bet of $10 wins $12.

In case of a win, the payoff is made by the dealer, who places the chips next to the initial bets.

Odds bets decrease the House percentage take. If Odds bets equal in amount with the corresponding Pass line bets are taken whenever possible, the *House edge (as far as Pass line bets and the associated Odds bets are concerned) is about* 0.85%.

This is better for the player than Blackjack played with *four decks*, under the usual Reno-Tahoe or Puerto-Rican rules (assuming of course that the player uses the Basic strategy, which will be described in Chapter 3).

In a plush Casino, the lowest valued chip found at a Craps table is usually the $1 chip. For this reason the House cannot pay-off on any fraction of a dollar. For instance, if you play at a $1-minimum table, place a $3 Odds bet and win with a point of 9, you should be paid 3 to 2, that is $4.50. However, the rules of the Casino you play in might be such that you will receive only $4.00. In the long run, this substantially increases the House take. For this reason you should always place only Odds bets which are paid fully. If your bet is $10, or a multiple of $10, then you will be paid correctly, regardless of what the point is.

The Casino you play in not only might not pay-off on any part of a dollar, but might not even pay-off on any fraction of the minimum bet allowed at the table you play,

It is important to know what the maximum amount allowed for Odds bets is. This amount depends, of course, on the amount of your Pass line bet and on the rules in force in the Casino you are in. The most usual rules are discussed below:

Certain Casinos allow only Odds bets which are *not larger* than the corresponding Pass line bets (single Odds).

Other Casinos allow Odds bets which depend on the Point, and which may be larger than the corresponding Pass line bets (full odds), as follows:

When the *Point is* 4 *or* 10, the Odds bet cannot be larger than the corresponding Pass line bets. Notice that in this case a winning Odds bet is paid 2 to 1, and hence it can be paid correctly independently of its amount.

When the *Point is* 5 *or* 9, the Odds bets can be larger than the corresponding Pass line bets, as explained below. Assume that John plays at a $1 minimum table and that he places a $35 Odds bet. If he wins, this Odds bet cannot be paid correctly using $1 chips.* For this reason, he is allowed to place a Pass line bet of $35 and an Odds bet of $36 (36 = 35 + 1). In case of a win, this Odds bet pays

$$\$54 \ (54 = (3/2) \times 36).$$

If John places a Pass line bet of $27, then he is allowed to place an Odds bet of $28 (28 = 27 + 1). In case of a win the Odds bet pays

$$\$42 \ (42 = (3/2) \times 28).$$

If John places a $175 Pass line bet using seven $25 chips, then he may be allowed to place a $200 associated Odds bet. Hence he may be allowed not only to increase the size of the Odds bet by one $1 chip, but even by one chip of the same *denomination* as the chips used for the initial bet.

When the *Point is* 6 *or* 8, the Odds bets can be placed as explained below. Assume that Sandi plays at a $1-minimum table. If she makes a $15, $16 or a $17 Pass line bet, then the largest Odds bet she can make is $15.† If she places an $18, $19 or a $20 Pass line bet, then she can make a $20 Odds bet. Hence she can increase the size of her Odds bet by at most two units. If Sandi's Pass line bet is $1 or $2, she cannot

---

*Recall that when the Point is 5 or 9, an Odds bet is paid 3 to 2. Obviously every bet consisting of an even number of chips can be paid correctly. Recall that 0, 2, 4, 6, 8, 10, 12, . . . are the even (positive) numbers.
†Recall that when the Point is 6 or 8 an Odds bet is paid 6 to 5. In this case the payoff of an Odds bet cannot be made correctly, using chips having as their value the table minimum, unless such a bet is made in multiples of five such chips.

place a corresponding Odds bet. If her Pass line bet is $3, $4 or $5, she is allowed to make a $5 odds bet. Again, as in the case when the Point is 5 or 9, Sandi might be allowed to adjust her Odds bet, using chips of the same denomination she used for the Pass line bet.

As a variant to the rule, if her bet is for instance $2, she might be allowed to place a $2 Odds bet. But then, in case of a win, she will be paid only $2 instead of $2.40. Still other Casinos, but only a few, allow the player to place Odds bets twice as large as the corresponding Pass line bets (double Odds).

As we have mentioned before, Odds bets decrease the House percentage take. In fact the higher the Odds bets are, the smaller this percentage becomes. However before we become too enthusiastic about such bets, we should observe that this does not mean necessarily that the *total* take from the player is less.

For instance, assume that Carol places *one hundred* $10 Pass line bets. In this case she will lose on the average 1.4% of $1,000, that is, about $14. Now assume that Carol decides to place Odds bets equal in amount to the corresponding Pass line bets whenever possible, and that such bets are paid correctly in case of a win. On the average, two of three Come-out rolls establish a Point. Hence, the total amount of money Carol will place on the table will be about

$$\$1,000 + \tfrac{2}{3} \times \$1,000 = \text{about } \$1,666.$$

Now 0.85% of $1,666 is about $14. Hence the House take is *the same as before*.

The above discussion shows that on the average, the player who places one hundred $10 Pass line bets loses about the same as the player who places one hundred $10 Pass line bets and takes the Odds whenever possible. Of course the player who places one hundred $10 Pass line bets and takes the Odds whenever possible is better off than the player who places one hundred $20 Pass line bets and *does not take the Odds.*

Odds bets associated with Pass line bets can be removed before any roll of the dice.

ODDS BETS AND COME BETS (TAKING THE ODDS)

A player who makes a *Come bet* is allowed to place an additional bet (associated with the Come bet) called again an Odds bet, as soon as a Point is established for the Come bet.

The size of Odds bets associated with Come bets is governed by the same rules that govern the size of Odds bets associated with Pass line bets. The payoff for Odds bets associated with Come bets is again the same as in the case of Odds bets associated with Pass line bets.

Assume that Sandi plays at a $1-minimum table and places a $10 Come bet. If the outcome of the next roll is, for instance 5, then 5 becomes the Point for Sandi's Come bet. The dealer will move her Come bet to one of the Point boxes marked by the number 5. Sandi may make now, if she wishes, an Odds bet associated with the Come bet. For this she will usually place the chips on the table (or alternatively she may hand the chips to the dealer) and say, *Odds on 5*. The dealer will then place the chips as indicated in the figure below.

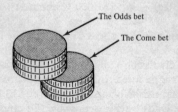

The Odds bet

The Come bet

Fig. 6

Sandi's bets will remain on the layout until the outcome is *either* 7 *or* 5. If 7 is rolled *before* 5, she loses both the Come bet and the Odds bet. If 5 is rolled *before* 7, Sandi will win. The Come bet wins even money, but the associated Odds bet is paid 3 to 2. If the Point were 9, the payoff would have been the same. If the Point were 4 or 10, then the payoff would have been 2 to 1. If the Point were 6 or 8, the Odds bet would have been paid 6 to 5.

In case of a win, the dealer first places the payoff next to Sandi's bets in the Point box, and then the total amount is moved to the initial position of the Come bet.

The Odds bets associated with Come bets are *off*, that is, are ignored by the House (they do not win or lose) on Come-out rolls, unless the player requests the contrary. If the player wants these bets *on*, on every roll of the dice, either a small *on disc*, usually white, or one of the Point markers, is placed on the chips.

If Odds bets, equal in amount with the corresponding Come bets, are taken whenever possible, and are always on, the House edge (as far as Come bets and the associated Odds bets are concerned) is the same as in the case of Pass line bets associated with Odds bets.

ODDS BETS AND DON'T PASS BETS
(LAYING THE ODDS)

A player who makes a *Don't pass bet* is allowed to place an additional bet (associated with the Don't pass bet) as soon as a Point is established on the Come-out roll. Such a bet is again called an Odds bet. The Odds bet associated with a Don't pass bet is made by the player by placing the chips as indicated in figure 7.

Assume that Dick makes a Don't pass bet, before a Come-out roll and that the outcome of the roll is 8. Dick may now place an Odds bet. The dice continue to be thrown until the

Odds bet (six chips)

Don't Pass bet

Fig. 7

outcome is either 7 or 8. If 8 is rolled *before* 7, the player *loses* both the Don't pass bet and the Odds bet. If 7 is rolled *before* 8, the player wins. However, while the Don't pass bet is paid even money, the payoff on the Odds bet depends on the Point. When the Point is 6 as above, the bet is paid 5 to 6.

The general rules concerning the payoff on Odds bets, associated with Don't pass bets, are as follows:

When the Point is 4 or 10, the payoff is 1 to 2. This means that an Odds bet of $30 wins $15.

When the Point is 5 or 9, the payoff is 2 to 3. This means that an Odds bet of $30 wins $20.

When the Point is 6 or 8, the payoff is 5 to 6. This means that a bet of $30 wins $25.

As in the case of Pass line bets, Odds bets decrease the House percentage edge. In fact, the higher the Odds bets, the lower the House take. If Odds bets, equal in amount with the corresponding Don't pass bets, are placed whenever possible the *House edge (as far as Don't pass bets and the associated Odds bets are concerned) is about* 0.83%. This is about the same as in the case of Pass line bets and the associated Odds bets. In fact it is even somewhat better for the player.

The player should place *only* Odds bets which can be paid correctly. For instance, if Dick plays at a $1 minimum table, places a $5 Odds bet and wins with a Point of 5, he should be paid

$$\tfrac{2}{3} \times (\$5) = \text{about } \$3.33.$$

However, he will usually be paid only $3.00, and will therefore lose 33 cents. We notice that an Odds bet of $6 can always be paid correctly at a $1-minimum table, independently of what the Point is.

Casinos often allow Odds bets which are larger than the corresponding Don't pass bets. Some Casinos will allow Odds bets twice as large as the Don't pass bets. Others will allow Odds bets which, in case of a win, will pay an amount equal to the corresponding Don't pass bet. In this case the amount allowed for the Odds bets depends on the Point. For example, if your Don't pass bet is $20 then you will be allowed to place:

> An Odds bet of $40 if the Point is 4 or 10;
> An Odds bet of $30 if the Point is 5 or 9;
> An Odds bet of $24 if the Point is 6 or 8.

Odds bets associated with Don't pass bets *are always on*.

ODDS BETS AND DON'T COME BETS
(LAYING THE ODDS)

A player who makes a Don't come bet is allowed to place an additional bet (associated with the Don't come bet) which is again called Odds, as soon as a Point is established for the Don't come bet.

The size of Odds bets associated with Don't come bets is governed by the same rules that govern the size of Odds bets associated with Don't pass bets. The payoff on winning Odds bets associated with Don't come bets is again the same as in the case of Odds bets associated with the Don't pass bets.

Several more details will be given for the sake of clarity: Assume that Carol plays at a $1-minimum table and places a $10 Don't come bet. If the outcome of the next roll is 6, then 6 becomes *the Point for Carol's Don't come bet*. The dealer will move her bet to one of the Don't come boxes marked by 6.* Carol may now make an Odds bet. For this she will place the chips on the table (or alternatively hand the chips to the dealer) and say *Lay odds on* 6 or *Lay on* 6. The dealer will then place the chips near the Don't come bet in the same manner as in the case of an Odds bet associated with a Don't pass bet. Carol's bet will remain in the box until the outcome is *either* 6 *or* 7. If 6 is rolled *before* 7, Carol loses both bets. If 7 is rolled *before* 6, she wins with both bets. In case of a win the Don't come bet is paid even money, but the Odds bet is paid 5 to 6 (since the Point is 6).

The Casino edge, as far as Don't come bets and the corresponding Odds bets are concerned, is the same as in the case of Odds bets associated with Don't pass bets.

Odds bets associated with Don't come bets are always on.

PLACE BETS

Place bets can be made on

4, 5, 6, 8, 9 or 10.**

To make a *Place bet* on 5, for example, the chips are placed as shown in figure 8. Certain layouts (for instance in the Reno-Tahoe area) have special boxes for Place bets. A Place bet can be made or removed at any time.

Since the player might be unable to reach the area where the bets must be placed, the chips are usually put somewhere on the table and the dealer is informed of the player's intention. The dealer will then move the chips to the proper place on the layout. In case of a win the payoff and the initial bet are moved back in front of the player.

A Place bet on 9, for example, remains on the table (if not removed by the player) until *either* 7 *or* 9 is rolled. If 7 is

---

*See the footnote on page 13.
**These are just the numbers marking the Point boxes.

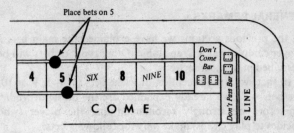

Place bets on 5

Don't
Come
Bar

Don't Pass Bar

S LINE

4 5 SIX 8 NINE 10

C O M E

Fig. 8

rolled *first* the player loses the bet. If 9 is rolled *first* the player wins.

> A Place bet on 4 *or* 10 is paid 9 *to* 5, in case of a win.
> A Place bet on 5 *or* 9 is paid 7 *to* 5, in case of a win.
> A Place bet on 6 *or* 8 is paid 7 *to* 6, in case of a win.

From the player's point of view, the best Place bets are those *on* 6 *or* 8. The House edge as far as these bets are concerned is about 1.5%, that is, about the same as in the case of Pass line bets.

The average overall House advantages, as far as all Place bets are concerned, is about 4%. If you make Place bets on 4, 10, 5 or 9 you should at least place them in multiples of five minimum table bets, since a win might otherwise not be paid correctly. Hence, if you play at a $1-minimum table, you should bet $5, or $10 (10 = 2 × 5), or $15 (15 = 3 × 5), etc. Place bets on 6 or 8 should be made in multiples of six minimum table bets (for the same reason as above). For instance, if you play at a $5-minimum table you should bet $30, or $60 (60 = 10 × 6), or $90 (90 = 15 × 6), etc.

A Place bet is *off* on Come-out rolls unless the player requests the contrary. If the player wants the bet *on*, a small *on-disc* is placed on the chips. Of course it would be *simpler* if the rules were so that such bets were always on.

GENERAL REMARKS

In the previous sections we have explained the main bets a player can place at a Craps table. Other types of bets will be described in the next sections.

In fact, with the exception of Place bets on 4, 5, 9 or 10, the bets we have already explained are the most *favorable*. Therefore we strongly recommend that the player (who decides to play Craps) make *only* the following bets:

> Pass line bets and associated Odds bets;
> Come bets and associated Odds bets;
> Don't pass bets and associated Odds bets;
> Don't come bets and associated Odds bets;
> Place bets on 6 or 8.

These bets will give the best chance for a winning streak.

While even longer winning streaks (for Pass line bettors) have been reported, we would like to mention that in July 1977, at the MGM in Las Vegas, one of us has observed a sequence of twelve successive wins. The probability of such an occurrence is less than 0.000206.

A player who places Odds bets associated with Pass line bets and Come bets is said to be *taking the Odds*. The player who places Odds bets associated with Don't pass bets and Don't come bets is said to be *laying the Odds*.

Taking and laying Odds decrease the House percentage take. We suggest, however, that you read again the end of the section explaining the Odds bets associated with Pass line bets.

Concerning these remarks, let us now assume that John has *one* and only one dollar left (this may happen in Las Vegas), that he wants to double his fortune and that he only knows how to play Craps (!?!). At a $1-minimum table he will then make, for example, a Don't pass bet. This is all right, but why is he not placing Odds bets, since by doing so he will decrease the House edge and therefore give himself a better chance? The reason is obvious. He cannot take or lay Odds, since for this he will need additional money. So when you place Odds bets it is true that this decreases the House edge, but you risk more money doing so.

Unfortunately, there are no systems for Craps which will assure the player of continuous winning. This is contrary to what happens in the case of Blackjack. All that talk about *money management* found in many books on gambling and about, let us say, *cycles* or *para-cycles*, is complete nonsense. More about this will be said when we discuss Roulette.

There are players who simultaneously place Pass line and Don't pass line bets of equal amounts. Then, if a point is established, they take or lay odds. These players believe that this way they play at least even with the House. Their *wrong* reasoning is as follows; The Pass line and Don't pass line bets cancel each other and hence the only significant bet on the table is the even Odds bet. Now it is true that the Odds bets do not give any advantage to the House. However, what these players do not seem to realize is that the Pass line and Don't pass line bets *do not* cancel each other. If for instance (6, 6) is rolled on the Come-out roll, half of the amount placed initially on the table is lost.

As we have already said above, a bettor gets the best chance for a winning streak by remembering the percentage of the bets allowed and placing *only the most favorable ones*.

There are some bets (which we shall describe in the next section), which give the House an outrageous advantage. For instance, *Hardway* 4 (this bet wins if you roll (2, 2) before 7, (3, 1) or (1, 3)) gives the House an advantage of over 11% (there are, in fact, even worse bets). This means that if you place ten $100 Hardway 4 bets you will lose on the average about $110. If you repeat this performance five times (and you can do it in less than an hour) you will lose over $500. It is a mystery why players place such bets—probably because most of them do not know what the corresponding percentages are.

At a Craps table the player always bets against the House. If the player wins, the win is paid by the House. If the player loses, the money is taken by the House.

All the bets we have described until now, with the exception of the Pass line bets and Come bets, can be removed at any time. All the bets we have described until now, with the exception of Odds bets associated with Come bets and Place bets, are always *on*. The Odds bets associated with Come bets and Place bets are *off* on Come-out rolls, unless the player requests the contrary.

At a Craps table, the dice are thrown by a player (the *shooter*) and not by a Casino employee. When a group of players arrives at an empty table, several dice (usually in a bowl) will be placed in front of one of the players. The player will pick two, and will roll these two dice until a 7 *is thrown on a Point roll* (if a 7 is thrown on a Come-out roll the player retains the dice). Then the player *loses the dice* and the player on the left becomes the shooter. A player who throws the dice has to have either a Pass line bet or a Don't pass bet. In addition, the player may place any other bets. A player may refuse, of course, to throw the dice.

The minimum and maximum bets allowed at a Craps table are usually, but not always, prominently displayed. This minimum and maximum bet may differ from place to place. On the Las Vegas Strip the most usual minimum bets are $1, $2 or $5, while the usual maximum bets are $500, $1,000 or $2,000. Several years ago these limits were somewhat lower. They have been raised to keep up with the inflation.

However, while the maximum amount is allowed for Pass line bets, Don't pass bets, etc., it is *not* necessarily allowed for other types of bets. For instance, it is not allowed for some of the bets described in the following sections which offer a relatively high payoff. Also, the maximum amount might not be allowed for Odds bets. The player who intends to bet high should request supplementary information concerning the limits allowed. Information concerning the amount allowed on Odds bets in relation to the corresponding Pass line bets, Come bets, Don't pass bets and Don't come bets, especially should be requested.

An outcome of 7 or 11 on a Come-out roll is called a *Natural*. The *Dice pass* when the outcome is so that the Pass line bettors win. The *Dice don't pass* when the outcome is 2, 3, 12 (Craps) on a Come-out roll or 7 on a Point roll.

BUY BETS (ALSO CALLED DO COME BUY BETS)

A *Buy bet* can be placed on any of the numbers

4, 5, 6, 8, 9 or 10.

To make a *Buy bet* on 4, for instance, the chips are placed in one of the Point boxes marked by 4. To distinguish such bets from others a small disc (marked *Buy*) is placed on the chips. (Come bets are moved to Point boxes as soon as a corresponding Point is established and, as we shall see below, Buy bets and Come bets are paid differently).

As in the case of Place bets, it is usually the dealer who places your Buy bet in the Point box. In case of a win, the payoff and the initial bet are moved back in front of the player.

A Buy bet can be made or removed at any time. A Buy bet is *off* on Come-out rolls unless the player requests the contrary (another example of a rule which has no logical justification whatsoever).

A Buy bet on 4, for example, remains in the Point box, until either 7 or 4 is rolled. If 7 is rolled *first*, the player loses the bet. If 4 is rolled *first* the player wins. The payoff depends on the number you bet on. If the number is 4, as in the above example, the bet is paid 2 to 1.

The general rules concerning *the payoff on Buy bets* are as follows:

> A Buy bet on 4 or 10 is paid 2 to 1;
> A Buy bet on 5 or 9 is paid 3 to 2;
> A Buy bet on 6 or 8 is paid 6 to 5.

Notice that the payoff on Buy bets is the same as that on Odds bets associated with Pass line bets or Come bets. *The House advantage as far as Buy bets are concerned is about 4.8%.*

To place a Buy bet, the player must *pay a 5% charge* to the House.* For instance if at a $5-minimum Craps table, Sandi wants to make a $200 Buy bet, she must place $210 on the table, $200 for the bet and $10 for the House (the *charge*). If the bet is removed from the layout, the charge is returned to the player (!?!).

Buy bets should be made in amounts so that the charge can be paid correctly. This is the case for instance if *the bets are made in multiples of 20 minimum bets.* If at a $1-minimum table you place a $20 Buy bet, a charge of $1 is levied. A 5% charge on $10 is $0.50. However, if you place a $10 Buy bet, the charge levied is going to be again $1 (of course this increases substantially the House take).

LAY BETS (CALLED ALSO DON'T COME BUY BETS)

A *Lay bet* is in a certain sense the opposite of a Buy bet. It can be placed on any of the numbers

$$4, 5, 6, 8, 9 \text{ or } 10.$$

To make a *Lay bet* on 6, for example, the chips are placed in one of the Don't come boxes marked by 6. To distinguish such bets from others, a small disc (marked *Buy*) is placed on the chips. (Don't come bets are moved to Don't come boxes

---

*A 5% charge on $50 is $2.50. A 10% charge on $20 is $2. A 5% charge is *half* of a 10% charge.

as soon as a corresponding Point is established, and Don't come bets and Lay bets are paid differently.)

As in the case of Buy bets, the Lay bets are placed by the dealer in Don't come boxes. The player will usually place the chips on the layout (or hand them to the dealer) and say, for instance, "*Lay bet on* 6." In case of a win, the payoff and the initial bet are moved back in front of the player.

A Lay bet can be removed at any time. The Lay bets are always *on*. Remember that Buy bets are *off* on Come-out rolls.

A Lay bet on 6, for instance, remains in the Don't come box marked by 6, until *either* 6 *or* 7 is rolled. If 6 is rolled *first*, the player *loses* the bet. If 7 is rolled *first*, the player *wins*.

The general rules concerning the payoff on a Lay bet are as follows:

A Lay bet on 4 or 10 pays 1 to 2;
A Lay bet on 5 or 9 pays 2 to 3;
A Lay bet on 6 or 10 pays 5 to 6.

Notice that the payoff on Lay bets is the same as in the case of Odds bets associated with Don't pass or Don't come bets. *The average overall House advantage, as far as Lay bets are concerned, is about* 3.2%.

To place a Lay bet, the player must pay a 5% charge to the House. *However this charge is levied not on the amount of the bet, but on the amount of the payoff you would receive in case of a win*. For instance, if you place a Lay bet of $60 on 5, you would receive $40 in case of a win. The charge you would have to pay is 5% of $40 (not of $60), that is, $2.

If you decide to make Lay bets, you should be careful and place only such bets which can be paid correctly and for which the 5% charge can be computed correctly, using the minimum value chips found at the table you are playing (see the section on Odds bets associated with Don't pass bets).

BIG 6 AND BIG 8 BETS

A *Big 6 bet* is made by placing chips in the area marked Big 6. A *Big 8 bet* is made by placing chips in the area marked Big 8. Big 6 and Big 8 areas are found at two of the corners of the Craps table.

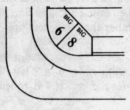

Fig. 9

These bets win if the number you have chosen (6 or 8) is rolled *before* 7 and lose if 7 is rolled *before* the number you have chosen. If you win, you are paid *even money*.

A Big 6 or Big 8 bet can be *placed* or *removed* before any roll of the dice.

The House edge, as far as Big 6 and Big 8 bets are concerned, is more than 9%. Therefore, it is about 6 times *higher* than the edge in the case of Pass line bets.

HARDWAY BETS

A *Hardway bet* is made by placing chips in one of the areas marked by

and located in the center of the layout. A Hardway bet can be removed or placed before *any* roll.

Assume now that Sandi places a *Hardway* 6 *bet*. The bet (if not removed by the player) remains on the table, until *either* 7 *or* 6 is rolled.

If 7 is rolled before 6, Sandi loses her bet. If 6 is rolled before 7, Sandi loses again unless 6 is produced with both dice showing 3. If the outcome is any other number, the bet is not affected.

Hence Sandi wins *only* if the outcome is (3, 3) and if this outcome is produced before 7, (5, 1), (4, 2), (2, 4) or (1, 5).

The other Hardway bets are settled in a similar way.

A Hardway 6 or Hardway 8 is paid 9 to 1, in case of a win.

A Hardway 4 or Hardway 10 is paid 7 to 1, in case of a win.

The House edge in the case of Hardway 6 or Hardway 8 bets is over 9%. The House edge in the case of Hardway 4 or Hardway 10 bets is over 11%.

The Hardway 4 and Hardway 10 bets are in fact among the best bets *for the House*. Some players are lured into placing Hardway bets by the relatively high (possible but improbable) payoffs. Other players place Hardway bets when 4, 6, 8, or 10 becomes the Point on a Come-out roll. Of course there is no justification whatsoever for this.

ONE-ROLL BETS

The bets described below can be placed any time the player wishes. Once such a bet is made, the *next roll of the dice* decides whether the player wins or loses.

Field Bets

A *Field bet* is made by placing chips in the *Field area*. The numbers 2, 3, 4, 9, 10, 11, 12, are marked there.

A player who places a Field bet *wins* if the outcome of the next roll is 2, 3, 4, 9, 10, 11 or 12. The player loses if the outcome of the next roll is 5, 6, 7 or 8.

The player who placed a Field bet wins *even money* if the outcome is 3, 4, 9, 10 or 11. The payoff varies when the player wins with an outcome of 2 or 12. Most often a win with such an outcome is paid 2 to 1. In this case *the House edge is about* 5.6%. When, for instance, a win with an outcome of 2 is paid 2 to 1 and a win with an outcome of 12 is paid 3 to 1, the House advantage decreases to about 2.8%.

Any Craps

Any Craps bets are made by placing the chips in the *Any Craps area*, in the middle of the layout. A player who makes such a bet wins only if the outcome is 2, 3 or 12, and loses otherwise. Any Craps bets are paid 7 to 1, in case of a win. *The House has an edge of about 11%.*

One Number, One Roll Bets

In the center of the layout there are areas where bets can be placed on *each* one of the following numbers:

7, 11, 2, 12 or 3.

For instance, a *Bet on* 11 is made by placing chips in one of the areas marked by

The player who makes such a bet wins if the outcome of the *next roll* is 11 and loses otherwise.

A Bet on 7 is paid 4 to 1, in case of a win;

---

*More precisely, it is about 11.111111111%.

A Bet on 11 is paid 14 to 1, in case of a win;
A Bet on 2 is paid 29 to 1, in case of a win;
A Bet on 12 is paid 29 to 1, in case of a win;
A Bet on 3 is paid 14 to 1, in case of a win.

Some more generous (!) Casinos will *even* increase the payoffs for bets on 2 and 12 from 29 to 1, to 30 to 1. Notice that since 2 and 12 are thrown on the average once in 36 rolls, the *fair* payoff is 35 to 1.

The House edge in the case of each one of the above bets is over 16%.*

Craps-eleven (or Horn Bet)

A *Craps-eleven* bet is waged in the center of the layout, as indicated below:

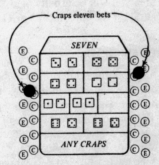

On certain layouts, especially in the Reno-Tahoe area, there is a special box for the Horn bet.

Fig. 10

When you place such a bet you win if on the next roll the outcome is 2, 3, 11 or 12 and lose otherwise. The payoff, in

---

*More precisely it is about 16.666666666%.

case of a win, depends on the number thrown, and on the Casino you are in. For instance, in certain Casinos (especially on the Las Vegas Strip) a Craps-eleven bet is paid 6.75 to 1 if 2 or 12 are rolled, and 2.75 to 1, if 3 or 11 are thrown. In this case *the House edge is over* 15%. In other Casinos (especially in the Reno-Tahoe area) a Craps-eleven bet is paid 6.75 to 1 if 2 or 12 are rolled and 3 to 1 if 3 or 11 are rolled. In this case *the House edge is somewhat smaller but still over* 12% (in fact it is 12.5%).

We notice that Craps-eleven bets cannot be paid correctly using minimum table chips, *unless they are made in multiples of 4 such chips*. Hence, only such amounts should be placed as bets.

For instance, if you play on the Las Vegas Strip at a $1-minimum table and place a $4 Horn bet, you will be paid $27 if the outcome is 2 or 12 and $11 if the outcome is 3 or 11. In the Reno-Tahoe area you will be usually paid $27 if the outcome is 2 or 12, but $12 if the outcome is 3 or 11.

CONCLUDING REMARKS

Certain Casinos allow various other types of bets, different from the ones we have explained until now. However, all these bets give the House a very high edge, do not present any interest for the player and therefore will not be considered here. As we have already said, the best strategy for the player who wants to have a winning streak is to place only those bets which have the lowest percentage.

We recall that Big 6 bets *win* if 6 is rolled *before* 7 and *lose* if 7 is rolled *before* 6. Big 8 bets win and lose the same way. If you win with Big 6 or Big 8 bets you win even money. The House edge as far as these bets are concerned is over 9%. Now recall that Place bets on 6 and 8 win and lose the same way. If you win with such Place bets you are paid 7 to 6. The House edge as far as these bets are concerned is about 1.5% (that is, about six times smaller than in the case of Big 6 and

Big 8 bets). In view of the above, why in the world do so many players continue to make Big 6 and Big 8 bets, instead of the corresponding Place bets?

We close this section by observing that the calculations necessary for obtaining the percentages given for the various types of bets which can be placed at a Craps table are not really difficult. In any case the rigorous setting of some of these computations require the use of "infinite products of probability spaces." Most of the calculations concerning Blackjack are even harder to set up and perform. In this volume we do not intend to burden the reader with theoretical considerations. We have however gathered several relatively simple computations in an appendix at the end of the volume.

BEST BETS AT A CRAPS TABLE

PASS LINE BETS

PASS LINE BETS AND ODDS BETS

COME BETS

COME BETS AND ODDS BETS

DON'T PASS BETS

DON'T PASS BETS AND ODDS BETS

DON'T COME BETS

DON'T COME BETS AND ODDS BETS

PLACE BETS ON 6 OR 8

Odds bets should be taken and laid, *no matter what the Point is*.

It is substantially better to place one hundred $10 Pass line bets and take Odds whenever possible, than to place one hundred $20 Pass line bets.

Place only Odds bets which can be paid *correctly*. If you do not realize immediately what you should bet, ask one of the dealers what the maximum amount you may place (as an Odds bet) is, in relation to your Pass line bet, or Don't pass bet, etc.

Place only Place bets which can be paid *correctly*. Remember that Place bets on 6 and 8 are paid 7 to 6. Hence, at a $1-minimum table, your Place bets on 6 and 8 should be made in multiples of $6, that is $6, $12, $18, $24, etc.

When you place a Come bet, don't let it be moved to "the previous Point," no matter what the Point is.

Remember that a Pass line bet is about 8 times more favorable than a Hardway 4 bet. It is about 11 times more favorable than a bet on 7, for instance.

Among the bets listed above the Place bets are the least favorable.

2
ROULETTE

Roulette is played at a table with a *wheel* and a *betting area*, like the one sketched in Fig. 2.*

There are 38 symbols on the circumference of the wheel, namely

$$1, 2, 3, \ldots, 36, 0 \text{ and } 00.$$

and for each one of these symbols a corresponding *pocket*. Except for 0 and 00, which are usually marked on a *green* background, the other symbols are on a background alternately *red* and *black*. In Fig. 1, the shaded area corresponds to the black background. The nonshaded area (with the exception of the squares around 0 and 00) corresponds to the red background.

The wheel *rotates* around a vertical axis and is located in a shallow bowl with a wall curved towards the inside. The wheel and the bowl are so designed that a *small ball* can be spun on the inside of the wall, without flying outside, and such that after several rotations the ball will finally *drop* into one of the pockets.**

It serves no practical purpose, even for the player who has never seen a

---

*The betting area is illustrated in more detail in later figures.

**Instead of saying that the ball landed in the pocket corresponding, for example, to 6, we shall often say that *the ball landed on* 6.

Roulette table, to describe further the shape and construction of the wheel. The above details are enough to identify such a table. Once this is done, several moments of observation of the game will give more information about the wheel and the way the ball is spun, than numerous drawings and lengthy descriptions. The player should however fully understand where and how the bets are placed at a

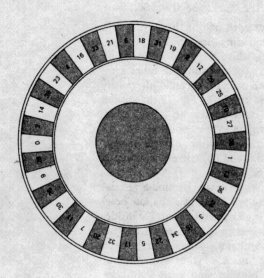

Fig. 1

Roulette table and the percentages corresponding to these bets (this will be explained further below).

One or two Casino employees (called dealers or croupiers) direct the game at a Roulette table. The wheel is given a push in one direction and the ball is *spun* in the opposite direction. If the ball drops, for example, on 9, we say that *the outcome of the spin is* 9.

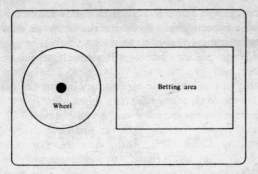

Fig. 2

Some tables have two betting areas with the wheel placed in between. Such tables are worked by two or three dealers. Both betting areas, or only one, may be open, depending on how many players are at the table.

Some Roulette wheels have only the 37 symbols 1, 2, . . . , 36, 0 and 37 corresponding pockets. We say that such wheels have only *one zero* and that the wheels with 38 symbols have *two zeros* (0 and 00). The game is substantially more favorable for the player when the wheel has only one zero. Unfortunately, almost all Roulette wheels found in North American Casinos have two zeros (more details concerning this matter will be given later).

ROULETTE BETS

Roulette bets are made by placing chips, or even currency, in certain parts of the betting area.

Once the ball, spun by the dealer, lands in one of the pockets on the circumference of the wheel, every bet on the layout *either wins or loses*. Of course, this depends on the outcome of the spin.

The players may place *new bets* as soon as the previous

bets are removed and until several moments before the ball drops in a pocket. Thus you may make bets even after the ball has been spun. However, how long you will be allowed to wait before placing your bet will generally depend on the dealer.

When you make a bet using currency one of the dealers will often remove it and replace it by chips.

Two types of chips are allowed at a Roulette table.

First, the usual *Casino chips*, the same as you use at a Blackjack or Craps table. These chips have their value marked on them and can be exchanged for cash at the Cashier's cage.

Then, we have the special *Roulette chips*. These chips have *all* the same size and design, but may be of different colors. In fact, on each table close to the wheel we can see several sets of chips of different colors. *No two players at the same table may have Roulette chips of the same color*.

You buy Roulette chips at the table you want to play. They are usually sold in stacks of twenty. It is *important* to remember that these chips cannot be used anywhere else in the Casino, except at the table where you bought them, and that they cannot be cashed at the Cashier's cage. Hence, when you finish playing you should exchange the Roulette chips (if you have any left (!)) for regular Casino chips, at *the same table* where you gambled.

The reason for the above is that Roulette chips have no value marked on them. They have a value when used in play, of course, but their value is determined at the player's request, in the following way: Assume that Sandi arrives at a table and asks for twenty, $1 Roulette chips. One of the dealers will hand her a stack of twenty chips *all of the same color*, for instance *red* (remember that no two players at the table have chips of the same color). Sandi will pay $20 for the stack. Then the dealer will place a disc marked by $1 (or 1) in the rack where the red chips are kept, or on a red chip. This way the House knows at all times the value of each red chip used at the table (during that period) and therefore knows how to exchange these chips if the player requests it. If Sandi wants, let us say, twenty more $0.25 chips, she will be given a stack of chips in a color different from red (their value will be noted in a similar manner).

Every Roulette table has a *minimum* and a *maximum* bet limit. Since these limits depend on the type of bets we place, it will be easier to explain them later.

Except for small variations in the design, the *betting area* looks like the one in the figure below.

	0													00	

		3	6	9	12	15	18	21	24	27	30	33	36	3rd	
		2	5	8	11	14	17	20	23	26	29	32	35	2nd	COLUMNS
		1	4	7	10	13	16	19	22	25	28	31	34	1st	
		1st 12				2nd 12				3rd 12					
		1 to 18		EVEN		RED		BLACK		ODD		19 to 36			

Fig. 3

There are *eleven* different main types of bets a player can make at a Roulette table. To facilitate their description we shall distinguish between *Inside bets* and *Outside bets*. The Inside bets are those which can be made by placing chips in the shaded area (see Fig. 4). The Outside bets are placed in the nonshaded area (see Fig. 4).

Inside Bets

We shall explain the *Inside bets* using the diagrams in Figs. 5 and 6.

43

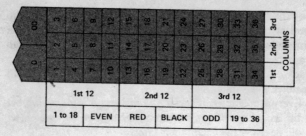

Fig. 4

Fig. 5

Single number bets. A *single number bet* is made by placing chips in one of the boxes marked by the symbols 1, 2, . . . , 36, 0 or 00. For example, *the disk labeled* R in Fig. 5 represents a single number bet on 32. There are 37 other such bets the player can make, including single number bets on 0 and 00. *A single number bet*, for instance on 32, wins if the ball lands on 32 and loses otherwise.

A single number bet is paid 35 *to* 1, in case of a win. Hence, if Sandi placed a $5, single number bet and won, the House will pay $175, so that she will collect (her bet included) $180 in all.

Two numbers bets (or Split bets). A *Two numbers bet* is made by placing chips on a line separating two boxes. *The disks labeled* B in Fig. 5, represent Two number bets, placed respectively on

$$27 \; or \; 30, \quad 1 \; or \; 0, \quad 2 \; or \; 00.$$

A *Two numbers bet*, for instance the one on 27 *or* 30, *wins* if the ball lands *either on* 27 *or on* 30 and loses otherwise.

A Two numbers bet is paid 17 *to* 1 *in case of a win.*

Among other Two numbers bets, we mention those on 0 *or* 00, 2 *or* 0 *and* 3 *or* 00. Of course there are many *other* Two numbers bets. We notice that, for example, we *cannot* place a Two numbers bet on 14 *or* 35, or on 14 *or* 18. But we may place the Two numbers bets 14 *or* 11, 14 *or* 15, 14 *or* 17 and 14 *or* 13.

Three numbers bets. *The black disks* in Fig. 6 represent *Three numbers bets*. Notice that there are in all fifteen such

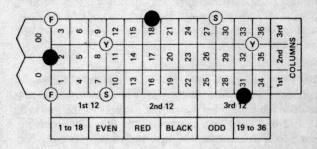

Fig. 6

bets. In fact, there are twelve possible Three numbers bets, corresponding to the twelve three numbers rows and in addition the Three numbers bets:

$$0, 1, 2 \quad 0, 2, 00 \quad 2, 00, 3.$$

A *Three numbers bet*, for instance the one on 7, 8, 9, *wins* if the ball lands *on* 7, *on* 8 *or on* 9, and loses otherwise.

A *Three numbers bet is paid* 11 *to* 1 *in case of a win*. Hence, if Carol placed a $1.50 Three numbers bet and won, the House would pay 11 × 1.50, that is, $16.50, so that she would collect in all (her bet included) $18.

Four number bets. A *Four numbers bet* is made by placing chips in the middle of a square formed by any four numbers. For example, *the disks labeled* Y in Fig. 6 represent Four numbers bets. A *Four numbers bet,* for instance, the one on 2, 3, 5, 6, *wins* if the ball lands *on* 2, *on* 3, *on* 5 *or on* 6, and loses otherwise. *A Four numbers bet is paid* 8 *to* 1, *in case of a win*.

Six numbers bets. *The disks labeled* S in Fig 6 represent *Six numbers bets*. A *Six numbers bet*, for instance, the one on 7, 8, 9, 10, 11, 12, *wins* if the ball drops on one of these six numbers and loses otherwise. *A Six numbers bet is paid* 5 *to* 1 in case of a win.

The Five numbers bet. *The disks labeled* F in Fig. 6 represent *the only Five numbers bet* which can be placed at a Roulette table. This bet *wins* if the outcome of the spin is 0, 00, 1, 2 or 3, and loses otherwise. *The Five numbers bet is paid* 6 *to* 1, *in case of a win*. Percentagewise, *this is the best Roulette bet for the House* (see the section on percentages).

Outside Bets

We shall explain the Outside bets using the diagram in Fig. 7.

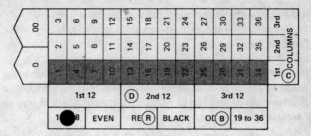

Fig. 7

Section bets (or bets on dozens). *Section bets* are made by placing the chips in one of the boxes marked by

1st 12 (1st dozen), 2nd 12 (2nd dozen), or 3rd 12 (3rd dozen).

The disk labeled D in Fig 7 represents a Section bet on the 2nd dozen. This bet wins if the outcome of the spin is one of the numbers 13 *to* 24, and loses otherwise.

A Section bet placed on the box marked 1st 12, *wins* if the outcome of the spin is one of the numbers 1 *to* 12 and loses otherwise. A Section bet placed in the box marked 3rd 12, wins if the outcome is one of the numbers 25-36 and loses otherwise.

In case of a win, a Section bet is paid 2 *to* 1. Hence if Carol placed a $10 bet, for instance on the 3rd 12, and won, the Casino would pay $20, so that she would collect (her bet included) $30 in all.

Column bets. *Column bets* are made by placing the chips in one of the boxes marked by

1st, 2nd *or* 3rd.

The disk labeled C in Fig 7 represents a *Column bet* on the 1st column. This bet wins if the outcome is one of the numbers in the column which is shaded. By analogy it should be obvious when the bets on the 2nd or 3rd column win.

The Column bets are paid 2 to 1 in case of a win.

We notice that the Section bets and Column bets are twelve numbers bets.

Even-money bets. The three types of bets we describe below are the even money bets a player may make at a Roulette table, that is, *the bets which are paid even money in case of a win.*

Bets on Red and Bets on Black. The disk labeled R in Fig 7 represents a *Bet on red.* This bet *wins* if the outcome of the spin is a number on a red background and loses otherwise. A *Bet on black* is placed, wins and loses in a similar way.

Bets on Even and Bets on Odd. The disk labeled B in Fig. 7 is a *Bet on odd.* This bet *wins* if the ball drops on an odd number.* A *Bet on even* is made by placing chips in the box marked EVEN. A Bet on even wins if the ball drops on an even number.

1 to 18 Bets and 19 to 36 Bets. The black disk in Fig. 7 represents a 1 *to* 18 *bet.* This bet wins if the outcome of the spin is one of the numbers 1 to 18. The 19 *to* 36 bets are placed in the box marked 19 *to* 36. Such a bet wins if the outcome of the spin is one of the numbers 19 to 36.

Notice that the even money bets are all eighteen numbers bets.

PERCENTAGES FOR ROULETTE BETS

It is interesting to observe that *the House edge in the case of each one of the Roulette bets we have described above, with*

---

*Among the numbers 1–36, the *odd numbers* are

1, 3, 5, 7, 9, 11, 13, 15, 17, 19, 21, 23, 25, 27, 29, 31, 33, 35.

The even numbers are

2, 4, 6, 8, 10, 12, 14, 16, 18, 20, 22, 24, 26, 28, 30, 32, 34, 36.

the exception of the five numbers bet, is the same, namely about 5.3%**

The House edge in the case of the Five numbers bet is even higher, namely about 7.9%.

Remember that this means that if, for example, you place *one hundred* $10, Five numbers bets, you will lose about $80 on the average. If you place *fifty* $20 Five numbers bets, your loss will be the *same*. The loss will again be the same if, for instance, you place fifty $10 and *twenty-five* $20 such bets. In fact, the loss will be the same (that is, about $80) as long as the total amount of the Five numbers bets you placed is $1,000, and it will not depend on the size or the number of the bets.

The computation of the percentages we gave at the beginning of this section is easy and immediate. As an example, let us show how we compute the House edge in the case of the Three numbers bet 1, 2, 3. First we observe that, as far as this bet is concerned:

$$\text{the probability of a win is } \frac{3}{38};$$
$$\text{the probability of a loss is } \frac{35}{38}.$$

If you place a $1 bet on 1, 2, 3 and if the ball drops on one of these three numbers you win $11. Hence, the expected return on $1 is

$$11 \times \frac{3}{38} - 1 \times \frac{35}{38} = -\frac{2}{38} = \text{about} - 0.0526$$

Hence, the expected return on $100 is about -5.26. This means that the House edge in the case of the Three numbers bet 1, 2, 3 is about 5.3%.

Let us see now what happens if the *Roulette wheel has only one zero.* In this case there are 37 symbols on the cir-

---

**More precisely, it is about 5. 263157894%

cumference of the wheel, and, as far as the Three numbers bet 1, 2, 3 is concerned:

$$\text{the probability of a win is } \frac{3}{37};$$

$$\text{the probability of a loss is } \frac{34}{37}.$$

Hence, the expected return on $1 is

$$11 \times \frac{3}{37} - 1 \times \frac{34}{37} = -\frac{1}{37} = \text{about} - 0.027$$

making the expected return on $100 equal to about -2.7. This means that the House edge is 2.7%.* The same edge holds true for all other bets at a Roulette table with a wheel having only one zero (there is no Five number bet at such a table).

As we have said before, almost all Roulette wheels in North American Casinos have *two zeros*. However, European and South American Casinos have Roulette wheels with only *one zero*. In fact, these Casinos often offer even an additional rule concerning *even money bets*, favorable to the player. For example, assume that Carol places a *Bet on even*. If the outcome of the spin is the number zero, the bet is not lost. It is left on the layout "en prison." If the outcome of the next spin is an odd number, Carol will lose the bet, but if the outcome is an even number, the bet will be returned to her. If the outcome is again zero the bet remains "en prison" and continues to remain so until the ball drops either on an even or on an odd number. The rule works the same way in the case of bets on 1 *to* 18, 19 *to* 36, Red and Black. When this rule is in effect, the House take is further decreased.

It is quite obvious to any observer that in Casinos in this country, Roulette is a game much less popular than, for example, Blackjack or Craps. We do not believe that this is

---

*More precisely, it is about 2.702702702%

due to the fact that the House edge is so high when the wheel has two zeros. There is very little *direct* player participation in the game of Roulette, when compared with the players participation in Blackjack or Craps. This must be one of the reasons. One other reason might have to do with the fact that the interval of time between the moment the ball is spun until it drops in one of the pockets is quite long. At Craps you might know the outcome almost immediately, once the dice are rolled. At a Roulette table it takes so long to learn that you have become rich!

We are persuaded that there would be a lot of interest in a game of Roulette where the players could spin the ball themselves, even if this game were conducted at a table with a wheel having even three or four zeros, nicely distributed on the circumference.

MINIMUM AND MAXIMUM TABLE LIMITS

Every Roulette table has a *Minimum* and a *Maximum* bet limit. These limits may differ substantially from Casino to Casino. On the Las Vegas strip the limits most often advertised are $1 or $2 minimum and $500, $1,000 or $2,000 maximum. The lowest value chips that can be bought at such tables are usually the $0.25 Roulette chips.

The Minimum and Maximum bet limits are however quite misleading. For instance at a $500-Minimum table, such an amount may be placed *only* as an Even number bet. The highest bet a player can place on Columns or Dozens is $250. As far as the Inside bets are concerned, the real Maximum limit is even lower. The Maximum bet allowed on a single number is usually $25. We observe, however, that in case of a win such a bet will bring $875, whence more than the Maximum table limit.

At a $1-Minimum table, the smallest amount a player can place on an Outside bet is $1. Individual Inside bets of $0.25 are allowed but a player is usually required to make at least *four* such bets (hence the sum of the Inside bets should be at least $1). These four bets *do not have* to be of the same type. For instance a player may place one $0.25 Single number bet, one $0.25 Split bet, one $0.25 Three numbers bet and one $0.25 Six numbers bet.

In the Reno-Tahoe area and Downtown Las Vegas, the Minimum table limit is usually $0.50. At such a table, the player may purchase stacks of $0.10 Roulette chips. The lowest amount allowed for an Outside bet is $0.50. On Individual Inside bets, $0.10 may be placed, but the player might be required to make at least five such bets.

GENERAL REMARKS

Unfortunately there are no systems a player can use to become a consistent winner at a Roulette table. We refer of course to systems which are nothing else but certain betting rules, more or less complicated, which depend on the previous wins or losses or the previous outcomes of the spin. We do not mean that certain other practical methods could not be devised for beating the game (see the end of this section).

The most popular system, used not only at a Roulette table, but also in many other games, is the so-called *double-up system.* Since it is so often used we shall describe it and comment on it here:

Assume that Dick decides to play Roulette, to bet on red and to use the double-up system. He starts betting a unit, say $1, on red. If he wins, he makes $1! If he loses he will place a $2 bet on red. If he loses this bet also, he will place a $4 bet on red. If he loses again, he will place an $8 bet on red. If he *wins* now, he will receive $8.

Observe that Dick placed the following bets:

$1 (loss), $2 (loss), $4 (loss), $8 (win).

Before placing the $8 bet, Dick lost $7. But, with his $8

bet, he won $8 (recall that a bet on Color is paid even money). This of course compensates the $7 loss and gives Dick a $1 *overall profit*.

We notice, however, that Dick risked $15 ($= 1 + 2 + 4 + 8$) in all, to win $1, and that he could have lost the $8 bet as well.* All right, some gamblers will say, even if Dick loses this $8 bet, can't he double-up again, that is, bet $16 on Red? If he wins now, he will have lost

$$1 + 2 + 3 + 4 + 8 = 15 \text{ dollars},$$

and won $16, for a net profit of $1. And even if Dick loses the $16 bet, can't he double up again and again? He must win sometime! What is wrong with this method? Well, there is plenty wrong with it. One of the reasons this method does not work is that if Dick loses nine times in a row and doubles the bet after each loss, then his tenth bet should be $512 and such a bet is not allowed at a $500 Maximum table. Oh yes, the optimistic gamblers will again say, but you *cannot* lose nine times in a row. The fact is that you can very well lose, not only nine times, but many more times in a row. In fact we can show (we do not intend to burden here the reader with computations) that in the long run the player cannot avoid losing, no matter how the double-up system is used. We personally know a gambler who, in several evenings at Monte-Carlo, lost an estate by playing Roulette and trying to impress a young lady (he probably lost the lady too!). Among other things, the player was complaining that during one evening the ball dropped on *red* 18 times in a row.

Another widespread system is based on the belief that if, for instance,

$$A \quad B \quad C$$

are the possible outcomes of an experiment and if *A* was

---

*The probability of winning with the $8 bet is 18/38. That of losing is greater, namely, 20/38.

produced, let us say, ten times in a row, then the chance that the eleventh time the outcome will be either *B* or *C* (and not *A*), is *greatly increased*. The gambler "possessed" by this belief will, of course, expect that if at a Roulette table the ball dropped on red fifteen times in a row, then on the next spin the ball will, or at least should, drop on black. Now, independently of how many times the ball dropped on red, the probability that the outcome of the next spin will be black is the *same* as always, namely 9/19. The same gambler will expect that if at a Craps table, the Pass line bettors lost, say eight times in a row, the chance that the ninth time the Pass line bettors will win, is greatly increased. Again, independently of how many times the Pass line bettors lost, the House take as far as the next Pass line bets are concerned, is the same as always, namely about 1.4%.*

The same fallacy is encountered not only in gambling, but also in every day life. You hear, for example, television commentators making remarks such as the following one: "By the law of averages he was due to score; he has not scored in sixteen previous games." Now, if the words in the above sentence would be "put in a hat, drawn at random and written down as drawn" the sentence so obtained would certainly not make less sense than the previous one.

Some time ago one of us was on a San Francisco-to-Chicago jet. The passenger in the aisle seat started to say that he talked on the telephone with his wife in Chicago, before take-off, and learned from her that there had been a plane crash near Midway airport (in Chicago). Then, with a smile, he added: "We are now safe. Once there has been an accident in Chicago, the probability of a second accident in the

---

*If we toss a coin, say, eleven times, the following sequences of outcomes, for example, have the same chance to be produced (H = Head, T = Tail):

```
H H H H H H H H H H T
H H H H H H H H H H H
H T H T H T H T H T H
T T T T T H H H H H H
```

same town and same day is practically zero."

The probability of an accident of a scheduled airliner is in any case extremely small. However, the idea that the probability for us having an accident had to be even smaller, since there had been an accident that day already is a perfect example of *absurdity*. In fact, due to certain material causes, the contrary might have been true. For example, if the Chicago accident was caused, at least partly, by bad weather, the same kind of weather might still have been present upon our arrival and might have made our landing somewhat more difficult.

Such beliefs are to be found not only among average persons. For instance in *The Mystery of Marie Rogêt*, E. A. Poe writes: "Nothing, for example, is more difficult than to convince the merely general reader that the fact of sixes having been thrown twice in succession by a player at dice, is sufficient cause for betting the largest odds that sixes will not be thrown in the third attempt." With all the admiration we have for the creator of *Eldorado* and *The Raven*, we have to disagree with such a statement on two counts. First, many people *do* believe that if sixes have been thrown twice in succession the chance that sixes will be thrown the third time is greatly decreased; they do not have to be convinced. Secondly, this is not true, no matter how you want to interpret the experiment.

Until now we have always assumed that the game takes place at a table with a *perfect* Roulette wheel. If the wheel is defective, then certain bets might be more favorable for the player than others. For example, assume that the pocket corresponding to 1 is twice as large and deep as all the other pockets. It should be obvious that the ball will drop on 1 much more often than on any other number and that the player placing single-number bets on 1 should win. Of course, no Casino will use such a Roulette wheel or as a matter of fact any other wheel which has an obvious defect. However, a wheel may have various defects which, although not detectable directly, are enough to substantially influence the outcome (in fact there are many such wheels in Casinos). One way of finding such defects without any instruments is by taking lengthy data. Once we have concluded that for instance the outcome is 1 *more often* than it should be, it might be advisable to bet on 1. Whether or not it is advisable to bet that way depends on the frequency with which the ball drops on 1. On the average the ball should drop on 1 once in thirty-eight spins. There is no doubt that this method works, the only problem being the gathering of the necessary data.

3
BLACKJACK

Blackjack is a game played with cards, between one or several players and a dealer who represents the House. Roughly speaking, the goal of each one of the players is to obtain a hand having a value greater than the value of the dealer's hand, but without exceeding 21.

Within the rules of the game, which set forth what you can or cannot do, the player has certain options. For example (everything will be explained further below) assume that the dealer has a 7 face up and that you the player, have a 10 and a 6. The rules of the game allow you to ask or not to ask, for one or more successive cards. What decision should you make? In this case the answer is very simple. If you did not keep track of the cards dealt from the deck, then you should most certainly ask for one card.

Therefore we must differentiate between the rules of the game (which tell you what you can or cannot do) and the strategy you should adopt. There are slight variations in the rules of Blackjack, depending on the Casino you play in or town you are in. Also, the game can be played with one, two or more decks. Here we shall describe the rules most commonly used on the Las Vegas Strip. Certain variations will be discussed later.

THE VALUE OF A HAND. SOFT AND HARD HANDS.

To explain the game it is important to know what we mean by the *value of a hand* (or of a group of cards) and the difference between *soft* and *hard* hands.

The Jacks, Queens and Kings are called *face cards*. The face cards are always counted 10. The Aces are counted 1*. All the other cards are counted as their face values indicate. For instance

are counted respectively 5, 3 and 10.

The card suits (clubs, diamonds, hearts and spades) have no significance in Blackjack.

To simplify the description of the game, *whenever we say that a card is a 10, we mean that this card is any one of the cards counted 10* (for instance, a *Queen* is a Ten).

An Ace will often be designated by the letter A.

The hand

---

*Traditionally Aces are counted "1 or 11." This is probably the reason for the great deal of confusion concerning soft hands.

consists of a five, a ten and a three. The *value of this hand* is defined to be 18 (notice that 18 = 5 + 10 + 3). The value of the hand

is 25.

Notice that the hands we considered until now did not contain any Aces. It is somewhat more difficult to introduce the value of a hand containing Aces. To define the value of such a hand we proceed as follows: First, as we have already explained, each Ace in the hand is counted 1. The total value we obtain is called the *hard value* of the hand.

For instance the hard value of the hand

Fig. 1a

Fig. 1b

is 22. The hard value of the hand

is 11.

The *value of a hand containing Aces* is defined to be equal to its hard value *if this hard value is 12 or more*. If this hard value is 11 or less, then the *value of the hand* is

10 + hard value.

For example, the value of the hand in Fig. 1a. is 17, since the hard value of this hand is 17, and 17 is more than 12. The value of the hand in Fig. 1b. is 22 since the hard value of this hand is 22. The value of the hand in Fig. 1c. is 21. In fact the hard value of this hand is 11, whence the value of the hand is 10 + 11 = 21.

A hand containing Aces is soft when its hard value is 11 or less.* All other hands, whether or not they contain Aces, are hard.

Therefore a hand which does not contain Aces is always hard. A hand containing Aces is hard only when its hard value is 12 or more. Observe that the value of a hard hand containing Aces coincides with its hard value.

---

*Notice that if you add *one* card to a soft hand, the value of the hand you obtain cannot exceed 21. Hence you cannot "bust by drawing to a soft hand."

For instance

is soft and has the value 18 (the hard value of this hand is 8). The hand

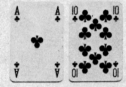

is also soft and has for value 21 (the hard value of this hand is 11). The hands

and

are both hard and have the value 17.

A *stiff* is a hard hand having a value of 12, 13, 14, 15 or 16.

The *9's, Tens* and *Aces* are called *high cards*. The cards counted 2, 3, 4, 5, 6, or 7 are called *low cards*.

THE GAME

The game is played at a table like the one in Fig. 2.

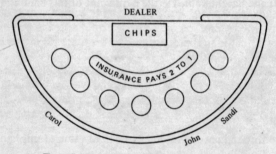

The small disks represent the betting areas. Rectangles or various symbols are often used for the same purpose.

Fig. 2

There are six or seven chairs for players and, on the table, in front of each chair is a *betting area*. The game can be played with one to six or seven players. It proceeds as follows.

Assume that there are three active players at the table, Sandi, John and Carol. Each player has some *chips*, bought from the dealer (or from the cashier's cage). Each one of the three players makes a bet by placing one or more chips in the betting area.

The dealer shuffles the cards and offers the deck to one of the players for a *cut*. If all the players refuse to cut the deck, the dealer has to cut the deck himself. The dealer places the first card at the bottom of the deck (*face up*) or in a box to his right (*face down*) and then he starts dealing.

He deals a card to Sandi, a card to John, a card to Carol (*all face down*) and a card to himself (*face up*). Then again he deals a card to Sandi, one to John, one to Carol (*all face down*) and finally one to himself (*face down*). Hence each one of the players has two cards (*face down*) and the dealer has also two cards (*one face up and one face down*). The cards dealt face down are called *hole cards*.

It is extremely important, *for the House*, that the players do not see the dealer's hole card. If the players always knew the dealer's hole card they could quickly win huge amounts of money. On the other hand there is no disadvantage for a player if her (or his) cards are seen by the other players or by the dealer.

A hand consisting of two cards, one of which is an *Ace* and the other a *Ten*, is a Blackjack (or a *Natural*). Clearly a Blackjack is a hand of value 21. Only a hand consisting of two cards may form a Blackjack. However if you have two Aces and split them (see below) and get a Ten on one of them, then this hand is not a Blackjack (it is not paid as a Blackjack).

When the dealer's up card is an Ace or a Ten, he must inspect immediately his hole card. If the value of his hand is 21, *then he turns his hole card up*.

If the dealer's hand is a Blackjack then he collects the bets of all those players at the table who do not have Blackjack (these players lost their bets). The players who have Blackjack (if there are any) *tie* the dealer. For instance if both the dealer and Carol have Blackjack, her cards will be removed, but her bet will be left in its place. She tied (or pushed) the dealer. She neither won nor lost anything.

It is customary that every player having a Blackjack faces immediately the hole cards (that is, the player places the two hole cards face up in front of the bet).

If, say, John has a Blackjack and the dealer does not, then (no matter what the dealer's hand is) John *wins* an amount equal to *one-and-a-half* his bet. Hence if he bet $10, he wins

$15, so that he collects in all (his bet included) $25. If he bet $1, he wins $1.50, so that he collects in all (his bet included) $2.50.

Assume now that the dealer does not have a Blackjack. If, say, Sandi does not have a Blackjack either, then she has the option of *standing* (not asking for additional cards) or *drawing* (asking for additional cards).

If she decides to stand then she places her two cards under the bet, face down, as in Fig. 3 (*the player should try to do*

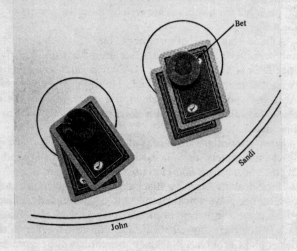

Fig. 3

this with one hand, and without touching the bet). If she does not like her hand, decides to draw and signals so (we shall indicate below how she should signal) then the dealer places one card in front of her bet, face up (see Fig. 4). If she is still not satisfied with the hand, then she may ask for further cards, which will be dealt to her successively, in the same

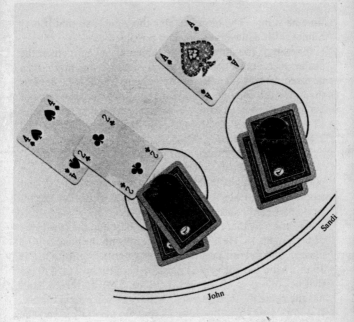

Fig. 4

manner. When she is satisfied with the hand and decides to stand, then she places her first two cards under the bet, face down. In any case if at any moment the value of her hand exceeds 21, then she should throw her hole cards on the table, *face up*. She *busted* (she lost) and the dealer will collect her bet and remove her cards.

Once Sandi has played her hand, the dealer turns (from his left to his right) towards John and then towards Carol, who will play their hands in a similar manner.

If all the players at the table have busted, the dealer collects all the bets, removes *all* the cards on the table and starts dealing again, *from left to right*, if there are cards left in the deck. In most places the dealer may shuffle practically any

67

time he wants. The house retains this option so that it may hinder skillful players as much as possible.

If some of the players at the table did not bust, then the dealer turns up his hold card. If his hand is 17 or more, then he is required by the rules of the game to stand. If he has less than 17, the same rules require that he draw until the value of his hand is at least 17 (he has to stand as soon as it becomes 17 or more than 17). Of course the dealer may *bust* (exceed 21) by drawing cards.

In some places the dealer has to draw on soft 17.

If the dealer busts, then he pays *even money* to all the players who did not bust. For instance, if John bet $10 and stood and the dealer busted, John wins $10 (so that he collects in all, his bet included, $20).

Assume now that the dealer did not bust and that the value of his hand is 18. He compares his hand with the hands of the players who did not bust (from left to right). For instance, if John's hand has the value 19 and he bet $10, he wins $10 (so that he collects in all, his bet included, $20). If John's hand has the value 17, then he loses. The dealer will collect his bet. If John's hand has the value 18 then he *ties* (or *pushes*) the dealer. In this case he neither wins nor loses. The dealer removes his cards but leaves the bet in its place.

Once the settlement is completed, the game continues as indicated before.

Other options the player has will be discussed further below. The most important ones are *doubling down* and *splitting*. A player may choose to play simultaneously as many hands as he wishes, if there are enough successive free chairs at the table.

The house establishes a *minimum* and a *maximum* bet for each table. In Nevada the minimum bets are usually $1, $2 or $5 and the maximum $500, $1,000 or $2,000, although there are many variations. In most plush Casinos there are tables having a $25 or even $100 minimum bet. The minimum and maximum bets are prominently indicated on each table.

Doubling Down

After receiving the *first two cards* the player has the option
of *doubling down.* If the decision to double down is taken,
then the *initial bet is doubled* by adding an equal amount
(placed to the left or right of the initial bet) and the hole
cards are placed on the table in front of the bet, face up. The
player is then dealt one and only one card, face down (see
Fig. 5). The player has now a three-card hand. *The settlement is made by comparing the value of this hand with the
value of the dealer's hand.*

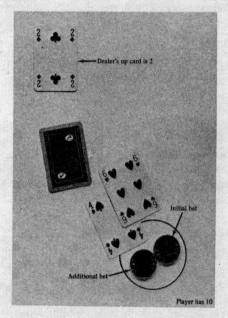

Dealer's up card is 2

Initial bet

Additional bet

Player has 10

Fig. 5

The player should not double on any hard hand of value

exceeding 11. Hard eleven is usually a very good hand to double down. Since there are 16 Tens in a 52-card deck, the player has a good chance to obtain a hand of value 21 in this case.

On the Las Vegas Strip the player is generally allowed to double on any two *first* cards. However in other places there are certain restrictions imposed on doubling down. For instance, in Reno the player is generally allowed to double down only on hands having the values 10 or 11.

Judicious doubling down increases the player's chances. When the player should or should not double down will be discussed in the section on strategies.

Pair Splitting

If the player's first two cards have the *same count*, the player has the option to *split*. For instance the player may split the hands

In some Casinos, the splitting of hands consisting of two 10's is restricted. The player is not allowed to split a hand consisting of a Ten, which is not a face card, and of a face

card or a hand consisting of two different types of face cards (for instance, a Queen and a Jack).

To split a hand we proceed as follows: Assume the player has two 8's (this is almost always a very good hand to split). If the decision to split is taken, then the two 8's are placed on the table face up, the initial bet goes on one of the cards and a bet of equal amount is made on the other card.

One card is dealt, face up, on each of the two cards. The player now has two different hands which he may play in the usual way. The hand on the player's right should be played first.

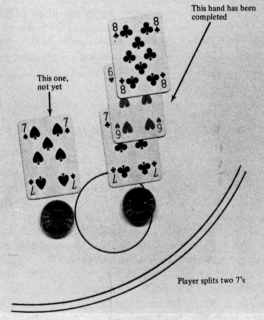

This hand has been completed

This one, not yet

Player splits two 7's

Fig. 6

In most Casinos a card is first dealt on the card to the

player's right. This hand is then *completed* in the usual way (the player may stand or draw). Only afterwards a card is dealt on the card to the player's left.

There is a significant difference however in the case of hands consisting of two Aces. In most places, in this case, *one* card is dealt on each one of the two Aces (as usual), *but the player cannot draw or split further.*

In very few places only, the player is allowed to double after splitting. For instance, assume that the player splits a hand consisting of two 8's and on the first one a 3 is dealt. The player has a hand of value 11, usually very good for doubling down. However, as we have already said, the rules of the Casino you are playing in may not allow doubling down in this case. Such restrictions increase the house take.

Judicious splitting increases the player's chances. When the player should or should not split will be discussed in the section on strategies.

Insurance

Insurance is a rule which is adopted in many Casinos. It works as follows:

Assume that the dealer has an Ace, face up. After checking the two hole cards, the player has the *option* of placing a new bet called *insurance* (in the insurance bet area).

The insurance bet can be at most half of the initial bet (and can be placed only if the dealer's up card is an Ace). For instance, if the player bets initially $20, the insurance bet can be at most $10 (here we shall discuss only the case of an insurance bet equal to half of the initial bet).

Assume, as we said above, that the dealer has an Ace up, that John's bet is $20 and that after checking his hole cards he decides to place a $10 insurance bet.

If the dealer does not have Blackjack, then John *loses* the $10 insurance bet. However, if the dealer has Blackjack, *then the insurance bet pays double*. In both cases, the settlement concerning the initial $20 bet is made *independently of* the insurance bet.

For instance, assume that John places the $10 insurance bet and that the dealer *has* Blackjack. If John does not have Blackjack, then he loses his initial $20 bet, but wins $20 with his $10 insurance bet. Hence in this case he neither loses nor wins anything. If John has Blackjack, then he ties with the initial $20 bet, but wins double, that is $20, with the insurance bet.

Notice that if John has Blackjack and places the insurance bet, then he will win $20, whether or not the dealer has Blackjack. However, if the dealer did not have Blackjack and John did not place the insurance bet then he would have won $30.

Dealers often show surprise (do they pretend?) when a player having Blackjack does not take the insurance bet. However the insurance bet is a *bad* bet for the player who does not keep track of the cards and *should not be taken* by such a player.

Unskillful players tend to insure when they have a good hand and not to when they have a bad hand. Probably they are influenced in their action by the usual meaning of the word insurance. They do not realize that when they insure, for instance, a Blackjack, they do not "insure themselves," but, in most cases, they insure the House against paying *one and a half the initial bet.*

Easy calculations (see the Appendix) show that if a player keeps track of the cards dealt from the deck, then that player should insure when and only when

$$\frac{\text{the number of Tens remaining in the deck}}{\text{the number of cards remaining in the deck}} \geq 1/3,$$

and this no matter how many cards remain in the deck (this result has been obtained first by E. O. Thorp).

Even the player who does not keep track of the Tens may derive from the above several simple insurance rules. For instance, assume that you play with *one deck* and that you are alone at the table. If on the *first round of play* the dealer has an Ace up and you play one hand only, then you should not take insurance no matter what your hand is. In fact, in this case you have seen only three cards. Therefore there are 49 cards left in the deck. Hence, since there are at most 16 Tens in the deck the fraction above is certainly less than 1/3.

In the same conditions, but if you play two hands simultaneously, and if there is no Ten among your cards, then you should take insurance. In fact, you have seen now five cards and none of them is a Ten. Therefore 47 cards are left in the deck and 16 of these cards are Tens. Hence the fraction is

$$16/47 > 1/3.$$

It follows from the above that if on the first round of play, the dealer has an Ace up and your hands are for example (4, 9) and (6, 8), then you should take insurance. However, if your hands are (10, 10) and (10, 9) or even (10, A) and (10, A) you should not take insurance. Surprised?

If you play with *two decks*, then on the first round you should not take insurance unless you have seen at least eight cards and if there is no Ten among them.

In the same way we may see that if you play with *four decks*, then on the first round of play you should never take insurance no matter how many players are at the table and how many of the dealt cards you have seen.

Surrender

An interesting rule called *surrender*, which is favorable to the player, is adopted in a few Casinos. Under this rule the player has the option of surrendering the initial two cards for half the initial bet.

For instance, assume that John placed a $20 bet, that his

hole cards are a ten and a six and that the dealer's up card is also a ten. If he wishes, John may surrender his hand (he throws his cards face up, on the table) and receives half of his bet back, that is, $10.

Usually, only hands consisting of the first two cards dealt may be surrendered.

Variations and Customs

In many Casinos Blackjack is played with more than one deck. In fact the number of such places is on the increase. When the game is played with more than one deck, the cards are often placed in a *box* (*shoe*) and dealt from there. In Las Vegas the cards are placed in a shoe only when more than two decks are used.

Under the *same* rules, the advantage of the house increases when the number of decks increases. However it is true that the dealer needs much more skill to cheat when a shoe is used.

When the game is played with more than one deck, the cards are often dealt all face up, except *of course* for the dealer's hole card.

Games played with more than one deck are usually dealt from two decks or four decks. Recently a number of Nevada Casinos started to use six decks (and to insert the joker very high). Since, as we have said above, the advantage of the House is increased in such a situation, it is hard to understand why certain players continue to patronize such places, *especially when they can find a Casino with four-deck games by crossing the street* (*maybe they like to lose their money!*).

We ourselves often prefer to play in four-deck games (instead of one-deck or two-deck games), but we do not see any reason to accommodate those houses which introduced six decks. For the readers who wonder why we prefer four-deck games we mention that such games are safer, *when the cards are shuffled well* (whether or not the cards are *really* shuffled is often difficult to ascertain).

In some Casinos the dealer is required to draw when he has a soft hand of value 17. He stands as usual on all hard hands having a value of at least 17 and on soft hands having a value of at least 18. Although the dealer may sometimes bust by drawing to a soft hand of value 17, this rule increases the take of the House. The player should avoid Casinos where the dealer draws on soft hands of value 17 (if he has a choice).

General Remarks

If the first two cards are given face down, the player should keep the cards in his (or her) hand as in Fig. 7. To signal that a card is wanted the player should *brush* the table lightly, for instance with the corner indicated by the arrow (see Fig. 7).

Fig. 7

The words *hit* or *card* can be used when requesting a card. If the player decides to stand, the cards are placed under the bet as in Fig. 3.

When the cards are dealt face up, then to ask for a card,

the player either scratches the table with one of the hands or points towards the cards. To signal that no card is wanted, the player may position the hand with the palm towards the dealer, as if to say "no more."

The player should try to make it certain that the dealer does not have reasons to say that he misunderstood the signal. If there is an important misunderstanding and if the *pit boss* (the dealer's higher up) is called to arbitrate, the player may take it for granted that the decision is going to be in favor of the House.

One early morning one of us was playing at a Casino on the Las Vegas Strip. We were dealt a hard hand of value 15. The dealer had a 7 up. The strategy we were using required us to stand (if you do not keep track of cards, you should draw in this case, without hesitation). While placing the cards under the bet, we were dealt a ten which busted our hand. The dealer pretended that he misunderstood our signal. It is true that we had to wait until the last moment, since we had to see the cards drawn by the other players, but otherwise it should have been *clear* that no card was asked. Since the dealer also had a hard 15 (and since the player on our left stood), he would have busted if the game would have been dealt correctly.

The player should also learn to count quickly both his (or her) hand and the dealer's hand. We remember once when one of us had a soft hand of value 19 consisting of a 2, a 6 and an Ace. The dealer had 18. While the settlement was being made a waitress brought us a cocktail. While we were tipping her, the dealer removed the cards and started to shuffle. When we asked why we were not paid he said that we had 18 and hence we tied. So our momentary inattention raised the cocktail to the inflationary price of $26.

Whether or not such mistakes are unintentional or intentional is of course irrelevant for the player who lost the money.

BLACKJACK STRATEGIES

In the previous sections we have described the rules of Black-jack. As the reader must have noticed, and as we have already said in the beginning of this chapter, the player has certain options within the rules of the game.

For instance, assume that you have two aces and that the dealer has a 9 up. By the rules of the game you may split or not split, as you wish. But what should you do, what is the best play in this case? If you do not keep track of the cards already dealt then you should split. However, if you do keep track of the cards the decision might be different. If, for example, you know that the remaining cards are mostly 2's, 3's, 4's and 5's then you should not split. In fact, if you split you will probably have two soft hands of value 16 or less, and there is a very good chance that the dealer will beat both of them.* Conversely, if you know that almost all the remaining cards are 10's then you should split.

By keeping track of the cards already dealt during the game and by correspondingly skillful play, an advantage can be gained over the house. In fact, Blackjack is the only Casino game for which *winning strategies* can be devised.

In one way or another, all such strategies require keeping track of the cards which are dealt. They also require varying the play according to the composition of the decks, that is, varying the amount of the bet you place, the drawing and standing strategy, and the doubling down and splitting strategies.

It is quite easy to see that when there is an *excess of high cards* in the deck or decks used in the play then *the situation is favorable to the player*.

Everybody can verify this assertion, at least in certain cases, in an extremely simple way. We proceed as follows: We remove from a 52-card deck several *low* cards, say a 2, 3,

---

*Remember that in most places you cannot draw further when you split aces.

4, and two 5's. Several hundred hands played (using the Basic strategy, which we describe below) with such a depleted deck, against an imaginary dealer will show that the player has a *substantial edge*.

Some of the reasons why the situation is favorable to the player, when there is an *excess of high cards* are the following:

There is a better chance, in such a case, that a Blackjack is dealt. The player and the dealer have the same chance to have a Blackjack. However, if the dealer has a Blackjack and the player does not, then the player loses the bet. But if the player has a Blackjack and the dealer does not, then the player wins an amount equal to *one-and-a-half times the bet*. The dealer and the player also have the same chance to receive a *stiff*, for instance a hand of value 16. The dealer *has to draw* to such a hand while the player has the option to stand. Hence, if there is an excess of high cards in the deck, there is a greater chance that the dealer will bust. There is also a better chance to form a good hand when you double down on hard hands when there is an excess of high cards. Conversely, when there is an excess of low cards in the deck the situation is, in general, favorable for the House.

In the next sections we present the *Basic strategy* first, and then two winning strategies, the *Simple count strategy* and the *Complex count strategy*.

The *Basic strategy* is not a winning strategy. However, as follows from the discussion below, the player who employs this method plays about even with the House, at least in one-deck games dealt under Las Vegas Strip rules. In a game played with more than one deck the same player will have a very slight disadvantage. In any case, a player has a much, much better chance of a "winning streak" if the *Basic strategy* is used instead of bad play based on "hunches."

The *Basic strategy* does not require the player to keep

track of the cards already dealt. The decisions to be made depend only on the dealer's up card and the player's cards. The strategy will be fully explained in the next section (see Tables 1–4). In fact, the reader who is not interested in these generalities may proceed to the next section.

The remainder of this chapter, including the *Basic strategy* presented in the next section, centers around the *Complex count strategy*. This is a powerful winning method which can be used in games played with one or more decks. It is described in the last section of this chapter. The corresponding playing strategy, that is, when to draw or stand, when to double down, when to split, is given in Tables 5–8. Betting diagrams are also included. Various computer simulations under real Casino playing conditions were made for this strategy. They have shown, for example, that in one-deck games played under Las Vegas rules, with bet variations from 1 to 5 and with somewhat more structured playing tables, the player has an advantage over the House of about 2.6%. In a multiple-deck game the player's advantage decreases slightly (for instance in a four-deck game it decreases by about 0.5%).

Since we do not want to mislead our readers we hasten to mention that such a strategy is not a "secret" you may hear while having a cocktail, and then be able to rush to the nearest Blackjack table and become rich. The *Complex count strategy* is a method of play which the player must master fully in order to be successful. This takes time and effort.

Since the occasional weekend player may have neither the time nor inclination to study the *Complex count strategy*, we present the *Simple point count* (before the *Complex count strategy*). This is a simpler method, much easier to master.

It is difficult to estimate, but in all probability the average "strange method" player gives the House an edge of between 5 and 10%. This means that from every $1000 put on the table the House will take between $50 to $100. And observe that it is not hard to place bets totaling $1000. If you play two hours and bet $10 per hand, the total amount of your bets will be approximately $1500 (assuming that you are dealt about 75 hands an hour).

We conclude with several remarks concerning the Complex count strategy and Tables 1–4. If you do not keep track of cards, but if for each hand you receive you compute the Complex count corresponding *to that hand and the dealer's up card* and play accordingly, then the playing strategy essentially becomes that described in Tables 1–4. In fact (in the case of 4-deck games) it becomes *exactly* the strategy in Tables 1–4 if we assume that each hand contains only two cards. In any case, the differences are very marginal, and the two-card assumption does not affect the important decisions of doubling down and splitting.

Computer simulations have shown that in games played with one deck under Las Vegas Strip rules, the player who proceeds as indicated in the previous paragraph has a small advantage of about 0.2% over the House. In a multiple-deck game the same player has a small disadvantage. For instance in a four-deck game the Casino has a 0.3% edge.

We have written the Tables 1–4, as well as the soft-hands drawing and standing strategy, as derived from the Complex count strategy for *four deck games* (with the assumption that the player's hand contains only two cards). The reason for this is that the number of games played with more than one deck is rapidly increasing.

Of course, the ambitious player will not be satisfied with the Basic strategy and should study a winning method.

The strategy described in Tables 1–4 is essentially the same as the *Basic strategies* given first by R. Baldwin and his group and then by E. O. Thorp. J. Braun, L. Revere and A. Wilson (this is why we also call it *Basic strategy*). The most recent results of some of these authors indicate percentages of 0% and 0.5% (in favor of the House) for the cases of one and four decks respectively. The reason why our percentages are slightly higher is that in our simulation the composition of the player's hand was taken into consideration through the *Complex count strategy*.

THE BASIC STRATEGY

As we have already indicated the *Basic strategy* decisions are determined by the dealer's up card and by the player's cards. In fact, except for splitting, they are determined by the dealer's up card and by *the value* of the player's hand. You do not have to remember any of the cards already played. The Tables 1–4 mentioned before, are explained below.

Draw and stand. Hard hands. Table 1 is read as follows:

Table 1.

These numbers represent the dealer's up card

	2	3	4	5	6	7	8	9	10	A
17										
16										
15										
14										
13										
12										

These numbers represent the value of the player's hand

If you have a hand of value 11 or less (that is, 11, 10, 9, . . .) you *draw*, independently of the dealer's up card.

If you have a hand of value 17 or more (that is, 17, 18, . . .) you *stand*, independently of the dealer's up card.

If you have a hand of value 12, 13, 14, 15 or 16 you proceed as follows: You determine the *block* located to the *right* of the number representing the value of the player's hand and *under* the dealer's up card. If this block is *shaded you stand*. If the block is *white you draw*.

For instance, assume that the player's hand has the value 13 and that the dealer has a 7 up. The block to the right of 13 and under 7 is *white*. Hence in this case the player should *draw*.

Assume that the player's hand has the value 13 and that the dealer has a 6 up. The block to the right of 13 and under 6 is *shaded*. Hence in this case the player should *stand*.

Assume now that the player's hand has the value 12 and that the dealer has a 2 up. The block to the right of 12 and under 2 is *white*. Hence in this case the player should *draw*.

Some players hesitate to draw when their hand has "high" values. The table shows that the only correct decision is to *draw until you have at least* 17, when the dealer's up card is a 7, 8, 9, 10 or A.

Certain other players have the tendency not to draw when their hand consists of *more than two cards*. This is a mistake. For instance, assume that the player has a hand of value 14 and the dealer has a 7 up. By the Basic strategy the player should draw. Assume that an Ace is dealt. The value of the player's hand is then 15. The player should draw again. Assume that another Ace is dealt. The value of the player's hand is now 16. By the *Basic strategy* the player should draw again. It is clear that (during this round of play) this is the last time the player will draw. In fact once the next card is dealt, the player will either have a total between 17 and 21 (17 and 21 included) or will bust.

The decision to draw on 16 against a Ten is a close one. In fact it is closer than those of drawing or standing against A, 9, 8 or 7.

A more detailed analysis shows that in certain cases our

decisions should depend not only on the value of the hand, but also on the cards forming the hand. However these cases are marginal and will not be discussed here.

Draw and stand. Soft hands. The strategy for drawing and standing with *soft hands* is even simpler than that for hard hands.

If the dealer has for his up card

$$2, 3, 4, 5, 6, 7, \text{ or } 8,$$

then the player should *draw to any soft hand of value less than or equal to 17 and stand otherwise.*

If the dealer has for his up card

$$9, 10, \text{ or } A$$

the player should *draw to any soft hand of value less than or equal to 18 and stand otherwise.*

For instance if the player has an A and a 7 and the dealer has an 8 up, then the player should stand. But if the dealer has a 9 up, the player should draw.

It is a mistake not to draw on soft 18 when the dealer has 9, Ten or A.

Situations like the one we describe below may sometimes cause confusion: Assume that the dealer has a 7 for his up card and the player an A and a 6, that is, a *soft hand* of value 17. The player should in this case draw (notice that with a hard hand of value 17 you always stand). Assume that a Ten is dealt. Now the player holds A, 6, Ten, a hand of value 17. But this hand is *hard*. The decision of drawing or standing reverts to Table 1. Hence the player should stand now.

Doubling down. Players are allowed to double only on the first two cards. In some places, for instance in Reno, the player is generally allowed to double only on hands of value 10 or 11. These days players are allowed to double after splitting only in very few places.

With a *hard hand* the player should consider doubling only when the hand held has one of the values 9, 10 or 11. When the player should double with such a hand is indicated in Table 2 below.

With a *soft hand* the player should consider doubling only when the hand held has one of the values 13, 14, 15, 16, 17 or 18. When the player should double with such a hand is indicated in Table 3 below.

Table 2.

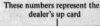
These numbers represent the dealer's up card

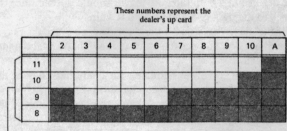

These numbers represent the value of the player's hand

Table 3.

These numbers represent the dealer's up card

These numbers represent the value of the player's hand

Tables 2 and 3 should be read as follows: You determine the block located to the right of the number representing the value of your hand and under the number representing the count of the dealer's up card. If the block is white, *you should double*. If the block is shaded, *you should not double*.

For instance (see Table 2) assume that the player holds a hard hand of value 9 and the dealer has a 7 up. The block to the right of 9 and under 7 is shaded. Hence the player should not double in this case. If the player has the same hand and the dealer has a 6 up then the player should double since the block to the right of 9 and under 6 is white.

If the player has a soft 14 and the dealer a 7 up, the player should not double since the block to the right of 14 and under 7 is shaded.

Notice that you always double with a hard hand having the value 11, except when the dealer has an Ace up.

Notice also that with a soft hand you never double if the dealer's up card is a 7, 8, 9, Ten, or A.

Some marginal cases are not included in the above tables.

Splitting. The strategy for splitting pairs is explained in Table 4 below, which should be read as follows: You determine the *block* located to the right of the pair representing your hand and under the number representing the dealer's up card. If the block is white, you should split. If the block is shaded you do not split.

For instance if you have two 7's and the dealer has a 5 up you split, since the block to the right of 7,7 and under 5 is white. If you have two 3's and the dealer has a 3 up you do not split, since the block to the right of 3,3 and under 3 is shaded.

Notice that you always split A,A and 8,8. You never split 10,10 or 5,5 or 4,4.

If you have two 5's the value of your hand is 10. You never split this hand. However if the dealer's up card is 2, 3, 4, 5, 6, 7, 8 or 9, then you double down.

Table 4.

These numbers represent the
dealer's up card

	2	3	4	5	6	7	8	9	10	A
A, A										
10, 10										
9, 9										
8, 8										
7, 7										
6, 6										
5, 5										
4, 4										
3, 3										
2, 2										

These numbers represent the
player's hand

General remarks. Above, we have described first the Draw
and Stand rules, since after all they form the most important
part of the Basic strategy. However *the player should of
course split or double first.*

The above Basic strategy has been presented for the case of
4-deck games. The same strategy should be used for all
multiple-deck games (except that, in the case of 2-deck games
the player should double on hard 9 against a 2 and on (6, 5)
and (7, 4) against A).

In 1-deck games the following modifications should be
made to the Basic strategy: Stand on (A, 7) against A. Split
(2, 2) against 3 and (6, 6) against 2. Double on hard 11
against A, on hard 9 against 2 and on hard 8 against a 5 or a
6 (except that you do not double on (6, 2)). Double on (A, 6)
against a 2. Double on (A, 2) and (A, 3) against 4.

WINNING STRATEGIES

In the next sections we describe two winning strategies. We present first the *Simple count strategy*, and then in the last section of the chapter, the *Complex count strategy*.

THE SIMPLE COUNT STRATEGY

To estimate the composition of the deck we associate:*

$$+1 \text{ with 2's, 3's, 4's, 5's, 6's and 7's;}$$
$$0 \text{ with 8's and 9's;}$$
$$-1 \text{ with Tens;}$$
$$-2 \text{ with Aces.}$$

We shall now introduce the *Simple count* of the deck, or more precisely, of the remaining cards in the deck by way of several examples.

Example. Assume that the game is played with a usual 52-card deck. Assume that the first card dealt from the deck is a 2. Since with 2 we have associated the number $+1$ we say that, at this moment, the *Simple count* of the deck is

$$+1.$$

Assume that the next dealt card is a 3. Since with 3 we have associated the number $+1$, we add $+1$ to the previous *Simple count* (which was $+1$) and obtain for the new *Simple count*

$$+2.$$

Assume that the third dealt card is a 6. Since with 6 we have associated again the number $+1$, the *Simple count* will be now

$$+3.$$

---

*The number -1 is read *minus one*, or negative one. The number -2 is read *minus two*.

If the fourth dealt card is again a 6 the *Simple count* will become

$$+4 (+4 = +3 + 1).$$

Assume now that the fifth card is a Jack. Since a Jack is a 10-*count card* and since with such a card we have associated the number –1, we *add* to +4 the number –1 (that is we subtract* from 4 the number 1) and obtain for the *Simple count* at this moment of play the number

$$+3.$$

Hence the cards dealt successively from the deck were

$$2, 3, 6, 6, \text{Jack}$$

and the *Simple count* is

$$+ 1 + 1 + 1 + 1 + (-1) = +3.$$

Example. Assume that the first seven cards dealt successively from a 52-card deck are

$$2, 3, 10, 4, 10, 3, 7.$$

The corresponding *Simple count* is then

---

*The numbers $+1$, $+2$, $+3$, $+4$, . . . are called positive numbers (the symbols $+1$, $+2$, $+3$, $+4$, . . . respectively $1, 2, 3, 4, \ldots$ mean the same thing). The numbers . . . , $-4, -3, -2, -1$ are called negative numbers.

Whenever we say that, for instance, to the number $+7$ we *add* the number -4, we mean that we *subtract* 4 from 7. Hence $+7$ plus -4 equals $+3$ (in symbols, $+7 + (-4) = +3$).

There is a little difficulty here for those not familiar with negative numbers, since sometimes we have to add, for instance to $+4$ the number -7. In this case we obtain -3, that is,

$$+4 + (-7) = (\text{to what?!}) -3.$$

The following examples will clarify the handling of negative numbers:

$$+4 + 3 = +7 \qquad +4 + 3 + 3 = +10$$
$$+1 + (-1) = 0 \qquad +2 + (-2) + 2 = +2$$
$$-7 + 4 + 3 = 0 \qquad -1 + (-1) + (-2) = -4$$
$$-2 + (-3) = -5 \qquad (-2) + (-3) + (-4) = -9$$
$$+1 + (-3) + (-3) + 5 + (-1) + (-6) = -7.$$

$$+ 1 + 1 + (-1) + 1 + (-1) + 1 + 1 = +3.$$

Example. Assume that the first four cards dealt successively from the deck are

$$\text{Ace, Ace, Ace, Ace}$$

(this is of course possible). The *Simple count* is then

$$(-2) + (-2) + (-2) + (-2) = -8.$$

If the next card dealt from the deck is a 6, the *Simple count* becomes

$$-8 + 1 = -7.$$

However, if instead of a 6 the card would have been a Queen, the *Simple count* would have become

$$-8 + (-1) = -9.$$

The simple count is determined in the same way if the game is played with two or more decks.

Since we have associated $+ 1$ with 2's, 3's, 4's, 5's, 6's and 7's, and since we have associated with Tens and Aces -1 and -2 respectively, it is obvious that:

I. When the *Simple count* is a large positive number, there is an excess of high cards in the deck used in the game. The greater the *Simple count* is, the more high cards are among the remaining cards.

II. When the *Simple count* is a small negative number* there is an excess of low cards in the deck.

In fact, if the *Simple count* is positive and large, we had to add many times $+ 1$ to obtain it. Hence many of the 2's, 3's,

---

*If a and b are two of the numbers

$$\ldots, -10, \ldots, -3, -2, -1, 0, +1, +2, +3, \ldots, +10, \ldots,$$

then *a is smaller than b if a is to the left of b.* For instance -10 is smaller than -5, since -10 is to the left of -5.

4's, 5's, 6's and 7's had to be removed from the deck and hence there must be in general an excess of high cards.

Conversely, if the *Simple count* is negative and small, we had to add many times − 1 and − 2 to obtain it. Hence many Tens and Aces had to be removed from the deck and hence there is an excess of low cards.

We should also mention that during actual play we cannot see *all* the cards which were dealt. Many players hide their hole cards, although as we have already mentioned it makes no difference (for them) if their cards are seen by other players or by the dealer.

Obviously, when we determine the simple count of the deck (or decks) we take into account only those cards we can see. The more cards we see, the better it is.

When we play, we sit at the table either on the first chair to the dealer's right, or on the chair immediately to the right of this one, so that we may see as many cards as possible. If these chairs are not available we just do not play at that table.

We shall now describe the strategy to be followed on the basis of the *Simple count*.

The Case of One Deck

The bet. You bet as indicated in the following diagram:

Bets	Simple count
1 unit	+ 1 or less
2 units	+ 2 or + 3
3 units	+ 4 or + 5
4 units	+ 6 or + 7
5 units	+ 8 or more

Hence you bet 1 unit if the *Simple count* is + 1 or less (that is, if the *Simple count* is negative, zero or + 1). You bet 2 units if the *Simple count* is + 2 or + 3. You bet 3 units if the

Simple count is + 4 or + 5. You bet 4 units if the *Simple count* is + 6 or + 7. You bet 5 units if the *Simple count* is + 8 or more.

Assume that the game is played at a table having a $5 minimum bet and a $500 maximum bet. The player may decide, say, for a $10 *unit* (bet unit). In this case, if for instance the *Simple count* is + 2 or + 3, the player will bet $20. If the *Simple count* is + 8 or more, the player will bet $50. When the maximum bet allowed is $500, the bet unit should not be higher than $100.

For each session of play the gambler should have available about 20-25 units. If you lose 20-25 units in one place and still want to play, we recommend that you go to some other place. We also suggest that you avoid the dealers to whom you lost 20-25 units.

You should remember that Casino owners are not too happy to see skillful gamblers at their Blackjack tables. They like to see you lose and lose quickly. *All that talk that it is good advertisement for the Casinos to have at least some winners is just "baloney."*

If you vary too often the amount of the bet, they will start watching you closely, to see whether you are using some superior playing strategy. Hence you should try to disguise your play as much as possible.

As far as betting is concerned the following is a *relatively* good idea: Assume for instance, that you bet 2 units and that you won. The dealer will pay you, whence there will be now 4 units in the betting area. If the simple count becomes + 4, remove one of the units, and bet 3 units. However if you lost and the Casino personnel is watching you, it is better to bet 2 units again.

Whatever you do, it is however doubtful that you will be able to disguise too much your play. There is a fool-proof method by which you will be detected. If you win several times in a row, or even once in a long session, everybody will know that you are a skillful player.

When the situation seems favorable enough you may place bets which are higher than those indicated in the previous diagram. You may for instance bet 5 *units* if the *Simple count* is +8 *or* +9, bet 6 *units* if the *Simple count* is +10 *or* +11, bet 7 *units* if the *Simple count* is +12 *or* +13, and so on. Therefore you increase your bet by *one unit* for every increase of *two units* of the simple point count.

In what follows a *notation like*

$$16 \longrightarrow 10$$

means that the player has a hand of value 16 and the dealer has a Ten up.

A *notation like*

$$7,7 \longrightarrow 8$$

means that the player has a hand consisting of two sevens and the dealer has an 8 up.

Draw and stand. Hard hands. You should follow the *Basic strategy,* with the following exceptions:

$16 \longrightarrow 10$ and $7,7 \longrightarrow 10$: *Stand if the Simple count is* +1 *or more and draw otherwise* (hence you draw only if the count is 0 or negative).

$15 \longrightarrow 10$: *Stand if the Simple count is* +4 *or more and draw otherwise.*

$14 \longrightarrow 10$: *Stand if the Simple count is* +8 *or more and draw otherwise.*

$12 \longrightarrow 2$: *Stand if the Simple count is* +4 *or more and draw otherwise.*

$12 \longrightarrow 3$: *Stand if the Simple count is* +2 *or more and draw otherwise.*

Draw and stand. Soft hands. You should follow the *Basic strategy*.

Double down. Hard hands. You should follow the *Basic strategy*, with the following exceptions:

11 —→ A: *Double down if the Simple count is – 1 or more.* Do not double otherwise.

11 —→ 9 and 11 —→ 10: *Double down if the Simple count is – 4 or more.* Do not double otherwise.

10 —→ 10 and 10 —→ 11: *Double down if the Simple count is + 4 or more.* Do not double otherwise.

9 —→ 7: *Double down if the Simple count is + 4 or more.* Do not double otherwise.

9 —→ 2: *Double down if the Simple count is 0 or more.* Do not double otherwise.

8 —→ 5 and 8 —→ 6: *Double down if the Simple count is + 3 or more.* Do not double otherwise.

Double down. Soft hands. You should follow the *Basic strategy*.

Split. You should follow the *Basic strategy*, with the following exceptions:

10,10 —→ 4: *Split if the Simple count is + 6 or more.* Do not split otherwise.

10,10 —→ 5: *Split if the Simple count is + 4 or more.* Do not split otherwise.

10,10 —→ 6: *Split if the Simple count is + 5 or more.* Do not split otherwise.

Remarks. The player should *master first the betting strategy, the rules concerning the cases when the dealer has a* Ten *up, and the first three rules concerning doubling down.* Afterwards the other rules may be learned.

We notice that on the average, once in every four rounds of play the dealer will have a ten up. In fact, the dealer will have a Ten up "once in every 52/16 rounds of play." Hence it is important to know what strategy has to be followed when the dealer's up card is a 10.

Insurance. The player should place the insurance bet only when the *Simple count is* +3 *or more.* The rule may be improved. For instance, if less than 39 cards remain in the deck, the player should insure if the *Simple count* is +2 or more.

Example. Assume for instance that the dealer has an Ace up, the player a 2 and a 3 and that the only other cards dealt from the deck (and seen by the player) are two 10's, two 4's, two 5's, one 6 and one 7. The *Simple count is*

$$(-2) + 1 + 1 + (-2) + 2 + 2 + 1 + 1 = +4$$

The player *should insure*, although the hand held (a 2 and 3) is a bad one.

Assume now that the dealer has an Ace up, the player has two 10's and that the only other cards dealt from the deck (and seen by the player) are a 2, a 3 and a 7. *The Simple count is*

$$(-2) + (-2) + 1 + 1 + 1 = -1.$$

The player *should not insure* although the hand held (two Tens) is a good one.

Further remarks. There is a certain pattern in the betting strategy, so that there should not be any difficulty in mastering it almost immediately. Also it should not take long to learn most of the several rules concerning drawing and standing, doubling down, splitting and insuring (the player should master *first of all* the rules concerning the cases when the dealer has a *Ten up*).

It remains to learn to count. Although this is the hardest part, the player should be able to count efficiently in several days, if enough time is spent on training. Count slowly, very slowly if necessary, and try to make no mistakes.

In fact we do not recommend a *crash program* of several

days for learning the simple count strategy. It is much better if every day, for a certain period of time, you read several times the rules and count once or twice four decks. You learn this way easily, without effort and without spending more than several minutes per day.

The strategy rules can be replaced by rules which take into account, at each moment, the number of cards remaining in the deck and other data. However, to master such an improved strategy would require an effort which we do not consider justified for the average weekend player. We have definitely observed that a player learns quite quickly and easily how to change the bet according to the count. Yet the same player will usually have difficulties in varying correctly the playing strategy according to the count.

For this reason we believe that the *Simple count strategy* presented above for one deck (and next for two or four decks) is the simplest and the best for the player who does not want to spend too much time on training. A strategy more powerful than all those mentioned above, but harder to master, is described further in the book.

Multiple Decks

The betting strategy recommended in the diagram on page 91 for games played with one deck, has to be modified in the case of multiple decks.

For instance in that diagram it is recommended to bet 1 *unit* if the Simple count is +1 *or less*, to bet 2 *units* if the Simple count is +2 *or* +3, and so on. Hence you increase the bet by 1 *unit* for every increase of 2 *units* of the Simple count.

In the case of a game played with *two decks* you should bet 1 *unit* if the Simple count is +3 *or less*, you should bet 2 *units* if the Simple count is +4, +5, +6 *or* +7, you should bet 3 units if the Simple count is +8, +9, +10 *or* +11, and so on. Hence, in this case, you increase the bet by 1 *unit* for every increase of 4 *units* of the Simple count.

However, once 52 cards are dealt from the decks, the player should again follow the strategy as given in the case of one deck. How do we know when 52 cards were dealt from the deck? Of course we may determine this by counting the cards as they are being dealt. If some players find this difficult (and in fact it is) it might be better to just estimate visually the remaining cards (it is surprising how precise such an estimation can be).

In the case of a game played with four decks, the Simple count required for increasing the bets should be even higher. In fact, in this case you bet 1 *unit* if the Simple count is + 7 *or less*, you bet 2 *units* if the Simple count is + 8 *but less than* + 16, you bet 3 *units* if the Simple count is + 16 *but less than* + 24, and so on. Hence in this case you increase your bet by 1 *unit* for every increase of 8 *units* of the Simple count.

Of course, when 104 cards (two decks) or 52 cards (one deck) remain in the shoe, you return again to the betting strategies recommended in these cases.

To simplify, we suggest that in games played with four decks the player uses the *Basic strategy* as far as drawing and standing, doubling down, etc. are concerned. However, the player should insure when more than 156 cards (three decks) remain in the shoe and the Simple count is more than + 12, when more than 104 cards (two decks) remain in the shoe and the Simple count is + 9 or more, and when more than 52 cards (one deck) remains in the shoe and the count is + 6 or more. Finally, when only one deck remains in the shoe, the player should insure if the Simple count is + 3 or more.

We leave to the player who decides to play against six decks (?) to determine the corresponding betting diagram and the Simple count for insurance. For drawing and standing, doubling down, etc., the player may use the *Basic strategy*.

In the Reno-Lake Tahoe area, the game is generally played with one deck, but the rules are less favorable for the player when compared with those adopted on the Las Vegas Strip. For playing in these areas the diagram on page 91 should be modified by adding +1 to the numbers in the second column. Hence, you bet 1 *unit* if the Simple count is +2 *or less*, you bet 2 *units* if the Simple count is +3 *or* +4, and so on. In Puerto Rico, where the rules are even less favorable for the player (and the game is generally dealt with four decks) the corresponding Simple count for increasing the bets should be higher. It should be increased by +8 if more than three decks remain in the shoe, by +6 if more than two decks remain in the shoe, by +4 if more than one deck is in the shoe and finally by +2 if only one deck is left in the shoe.

We close this section by observing that to win (with the methods described above) the player *must* vary the bet according to the Simple count.

Improving the Betting Strategy

Above we have recommended (for games played with *one deck*) a few changes in the *Basic strategy,* which are dependent upon the count. While these changes will certainly help the player, it is the betting strategy that brings most of the profit. THEREFORE TO WIN, THE PLAYER MUST VARY THE BET.

A large *Simple count* indicates a situation favorable for the player. However, how advantageous the situation is depends also on the number of cards left in the deck. For example a Simple count of +4 after 20 cards have been dealt is an indication of a situation substantially more advantageous for the player, than a Simple count of +4 at the beginning of the deck.

The betting and playing strategies can be improved on the basis of these remarks. Without going into details we mention that the various numbers appearing in the betting diagrams and playing rules, previously given, may be divided by 2 when less than 26 cards remain in the deck.

More precise strategies can be formulated using the Dubner-Thorp deck index D:

$$D = \frac{\text{Simple count times 100}}{\text{number of cards remaining in deck (or decks)}}$$

THE COMPLEX COUNT STRATEGY

In the *Simple count strategy* we estimate the composition of the deck (or decks) by associating

$$+ 1 \text{ with 2's, 3's, 4's, 5's, 6's, 7's}$$
$$0 \text{ with 8's, 9's}$$
$$-1 \text{ with Tens}$$
$$-2 \text{ with Aces}$$

When the Simple count is large, low cards are missing from the deck (or decks) and hence the player has the advantage. *When the Simple count is negative and small,* high cards are missing from the deck (or decks) and in this case the House has the advantage.

However, it is more advantageous for the player when 5's are missing from the deck (or decks) than when 4's are missing, more advantageous when 4's are missing than when 3's are missing, and so on. Hence a much better estimation of the advantage (at least as far as the betting strategy is concerned) will be obtained if with different cards we associate different numbers.

These are the general ideas at the basis of the *Complex count strategy*. We shall now proceed to explain it.

On the first line below we list the cards and *under each card we write the number associated with it:*

2	3	4	5	6	7	8	9	10	A
+2	+2	+2½	+3½	+2	+1½	0	–½	–2½	–3

We shall define now the *Count* of the deck (or decks). As in the case of the Simple count we shall explain what the Count is by several examples.

Example. Assume that the game is played with a 52-card deck and that the first card dealt from the deck is a 2. Since with a 2 we have associated the number $+2$ we say that (at this moment) the *Count* is

$$+2$$

Assume that the next card dealt is a 3. Since with 3 we have associated $+2$, we add $+2$ to the previous Count (which was $+2$) and obtain for the new *Count*

$$+4.$$

Assume that the third card dealt is a 4. Since with a 4 we have associated $+2\frac{1}{2}$, the *Count* will be now

$$+6\frac{1}{2}.$$

If the fourth card dealt is again a 4 the *Count* will become

$$+9 \quad (+9 = 6\frac{1}{2} + 2\frac{1}{2}).$$

Assume now that the fifth card is a Jack. Since with such a card we have associated the numbers $-2\frac{1}{2}$, we add to $+9$ the number $-2\frac{1}{2}$ (that is, we subtract from 9 the number $2\frac{1}{2}$) and obtain for the *Count* (at this moment of play) the number

$$+6\frac{1}{2}.$$

Hence the cards dealt successively from the deck were

$$2, 3, 4, 4, \text{Jack}$$

and the Count is

$$+2 + 2 + 2\frac{1}{2} + 2\frac{1}{2} + (-2\frac{1}{2}) = 6\frac{1}{2}.$$

Example. Assume that the first seven cards dealt successively from a 52-card deck are

$$2, 3, 10, 4, 10, 3, 7.$$

The corresponding *Count* is then

$$+2 + 2 + (-2\frac{1}{2}) + 2\frac{1}{2} + (-2\frac{1}{2}) + 2 + 1\frac{1}{2} = +5.$$

Example. Assume that the first four cards dealt successively from the deck are

$$\text{Ace, Ace, Ace, Ace.}$$

The *Count* is then

$$(-3) + (-3) + (-3) + (-3) = -12.$$

If the next card dealt from the deck is a Ten, the *Count* becomes

$$-12 + (-2\frac{1}{2}) = -14\frac{1}{2}.$$

The Count is determined in the same way in the case when the game is played with two or more decks.

Of course when we compute the Count of the deck (or decks) we take into account only those cards we can see.

Once the *Count* is determined, the next step is to define the *Complex count.* This is

$$\frac{\text{Count } \textit{times } 100}{\text{number of remaining cards in the deck (or decks)}}$$

Example. Assume that the game is played with a 52-card deck and that the cards

$$2, 3, 4, 4, \text{Jack}$$

were *dealt (and seen).* The Count is $+6\frac{1}{2}$ and the *Complex count* is

$$\frac{6\frac{1}{2} \times 100}{47}.$$

If the game were played with *four decks* and the same cards were dealt, the *Complex count* would be

$$\frac{6\frac{1}{2} \times 100}{203}$$

Example. Assume that the first seven cards dealt successively from a 52-card deck were

$$2, 3, 10, 4, 10, 3, 7.$$

The corresponding *Count* is $+5$ and the corresponding *Complex count* is

$$\frac{+5 \times 100}{45}.$$

It is somewhat more difficult to determine the *Complex count* than the *Simple count*. This is mainly due to the fact that the numbers we work with are either substantially larger or substantially smaller than those we encounter when we use the *Simple count* strategy and also to the fact that the numbers associated with the cards are not all integers.

We observe that we could multiply be 2 the numbers associated with the cards. The new numbers would now be 4, 4, 5, 7, 4, 3, 0, -1, -5, -6. However, these numbers are even larger in absolute value than the previous ones. For this and several other reasons we find it hard to use them in actual play.

The above remarks should not come as a surprise. The method we describe is very powerful. If it would be very easy to beat the game, there would be no more gambling Casinos.

When we play, we *associate* with the cards in the deck

$$2, 2, 2a, 3a, 2, 1a, 0, -a, -2a, -3$$

instead of

$$2, 2, 2\frac{1}{2}, 3\frac{1}{2}, 2, 1\frac{1}{2}, 0, -\frac{1}{2}, -2\frac{1}{2}, -3.$$

This increases substantially the speed of the counting. Of course

$$2a + 3 = 5a, 2a + 2a = 5, 3a + 2a = 6, \text{ etc.}$$

We shall now describe the strategy to be followed, on the basis of the *Complex count*, with the help of the tables below. We shall start by discussing the betting strategy.

The Bet. In *games played on the Las Vegas strip with four decks*, you bet as indicated in the following diagram:

· Bet	Complex count
1 unit	less than +6
2 units	+6
3 units	+10
4 units	+14
5 units	+18

Fig. 8

The figure should be read as follows: You bet 1 *unit* if the Complex count is less than +6. You bet 2 *units* if the Complex count is +6 *or more, but less than* +10. You bet 3 *units* if the Complex count is +10 *or more, but less than* +14. You bet 4 *units* if the Complex count is +14 *or more, but less than* +18. You bet 5 *units* if the Complex count is +18 *or more*.

The betting diagram for games played with *six decks* is obtained from the one in Fig. 8, by replacing the values +6, +6, +10, +14, +18, of the Complex count by +8, +8, +12, +16, +20, respectively.

In *games played on the Las Vegas Strip with one deck*, you bet as indicated in the following figure:

Bet	Complex count
1 unit	less than +4
2 units	+4
3 units	+8
4 units	+12
5 units	+16

Fig. 9

This diagram should be read like the one in Fig. 8

In the Reno-Tahoe area and Downtown Las Vegas, games are most often played with one deck, but the rules are less favorable for the player when compared with those on the Las Vegas Strip. In these areas (for games played with one deck) the player should bet as indicated in Fig. 8.

Further betting strategies will be discussed after we describe the draw and stand strategy, the double down strategy, the splitting stragy and the insurance strategy.

Draw and Stand. Hard Hands. Table 5 is read as follows:

If you have a hand of value 11 or less (that is, 11, 10, 9, . . .) you *draw*, independently of the dealer's deck up card.

Table 5.

These numbers represent the dealer's up card

	2	3	4	5	6	7	8	9	10	A
17										
16						+45	+40	+25	+1	+40
15								+50	+20	+50
14	−15	−25	−35						+40	
13	0	−10	−15	−25	−20					
12	+15	+7	+1	−10	−7					

These numbers represent the value of the player's hand

If you have a hand value 17 or more (that is, 17, 18, . . .) you *stand*.

If you have a hand of value 12, 13, 14, 15 or 16, you proceed as follows:

You determine the *block* located to the *right* of the number representing the value of the player's hand and *under* the dealer's up card.

If the block is *shaded you stand.*

If the block is *white without any number on it, you draw.*

If the block is *white and has a number on it, you stand if the Complex count is larger than that number and draw otherwise.*

For instance, assume that the player's hand has the value 13 and the dealer has a 6 up. The block to the right of 13 and under 6 is *white and has the number –20 on it.* Hence you stand if the *Complex count* is more than –20 (that is, –19, –18, . . .) and draw otherwise.

Draw and Stand. Soft Hands. When the dealer has 2, 3, 4, 5, 6, 7 or 8 up: *You stand on 18 or more and draw otherwise.*

When the dealer has 9 up: *You stand on 19 or more and draw otherwise.*

When the dealer has 10 up: *You always stand on 19 or more. You stand on 18 if the Complex count is more than + 15 and draw otherwise. You always draw on 17 or less.*

When the dealer has A up: *You always stand on 19 or more. You stand on 18 if the complex count is more than 2 and draw otherwise (in case of 1-deck games replace 2 by –10). You always draw on 17 or less.*

Doubling Down. With a *hard hand* the player should consider doubling down only when the hand held has one of the values 7, 8, 9, 10 or 11. When the player should double with a *hard hand* is indicated in Table 6. When the player should double with a *soft hand* is indicated in Table 7.

Tables 6 and 7 should be read as follows: You determine the block located to the right of the number representing the value of your hand and under the number representing the value of the dealer's hand.

If the block is *shaded you should not double.*

If the block is *white without any number on it, you double.*

Table 6.

These numbers represent the
dealer's up card

	2	3	4	5	6	7	8	9	10	A
11							−30	−20	−20	+4
10							−20	−10	+20	+20
9	+5	−5	−15	−20	−30	+16				
8		+45	+30	+15	+10					
7				+50	+50					

These numbers represent the
value of the player's hand

In case on 1-deck games replace + 4 (in the block under A) by –4.

Table 7.

These numbers represent the
dealer's up card

	2	3	4	5	6	7	8	9	10	A
20										
19		+25	+15	+10	+5					
18		−1								
17	+1	−10	−25							
16		+20	−5							
15		+30	−5							
14		+30	+2	−10	−30					
13		+30	+3	−5	−15					

These numbers represent the
value of the player's hand

If the block is *white and has a number on it, you double
only if the complex count is larger than that number.*

For example (see Table 6) assume that the player's hand
has the value 10 and the dealer has an Ace up. The block to
the right of 10 and under A is *white and has the number + 20*

on it. Hence, you double if the *Complex count* is more than + 20 (that is + 21, + 22, + 23, . . .) and do not double otherwise.

Splitting. The strategy for splitting pairs is given in Table 8 below, which should be read as follows: You determine the *block* located to the right of the pair representing your hand and under the number representing the dealer's up card.

Table 8.

These numbers represent the
dealer's up card

	2	3	4	5	6	7	8	9	10	A
A, A										−30
10, 10		+40	+30	+20	+20					
9, 9	−7	−15	−20	−25	−25	+30				+30
8, 8									+30*	
7, 7										
6, 6	+10	0	−15	−25	−25					
5, 5										
4, 4										
3, 3		+20	−5							
2, 2		+10	−5							

These numbers represent the
player's hand

If the block is *shaded you should not split.*

If the block is *white without any number on it, you split.*

If the block is *white and has a number on it, you split only if the Complex count is larger than that number.*

For example, if you have two Tens and the dealer has 4 up, you split only if the count is more than + 30.

The only *exception* concerns

$$8, 8 \longrightarrow 10.$$

In this case you *split only if the Complex count is* $+30$ *or less.*

Insurance. The player should place the insurance bet only if the *Complex count is larger than* 11.

Surrender. Surrender hard 15 and hard 16 (not (8, 8)) against 10 when the *Complex count is* $+1$ *or more.*

Remarks. In Puerto Rico, where the game is played, in general, with four decks and the rules are somewhat more restrictive, the player should use the following betting diagram:

Bet	Complex count
1 unit	less than $+10$
2 units	$+10$
3 units	$+14$
4 units	$+18$
5 units	$+20$

Tables 5-8 can be improved by introducing numbers in some of the white blocks, by replacing some of the shaded blocks by white blocks with numbers and by changing the numbers on some of the blocks.

Such modifications will improve the strategy of play but at the same time will make it much harder to master it. This is why we decided to present here what is, in fact, an approximation to the *Complex count* strategy. Complete details will be given in a theoretical book, to be published next.

As we have seen above, once we know the Count, the Complex count is determined by certain divisions. Since it is difficult to perform *directly* these divisions during actual play, we prefer to determine the Complex count by using

Table 9, below. Of course this table gives only approximate values, since otherwise it would have too many entries. In preparing this table we have taken into account, among other things, the *Basic strategy* and the fact that in one-deck games most of the hands are dealt, not from the middle of the deck, but from the upper half.

Table 9

[156,208]: $x \longrightarrow x/2$	[36,55]: $x \longrightarrow 2x$
[106, 155]: $x \longrightarrow x-x/4$	[26, 35]: $x \longrightarrow 3x$
[76, 105]: $x \longrightarrow x$	[21, 25]: $x \longrightarrow 4x$
[56, 75]: $x \longrightarrow x + x/4$	[11, 20]: $x \longrightarrow 5x$

Of course $x/2$ is half of x, while $x/4$ is one fourth of x.

To explain how the Table should be read we start by noticing that the values to the left of the arrows are Counts, while those to the right of the arrows are Complex counts. Denote now by N the number of cards *remaining* in the deck (or decks) used in play. If, for instance, the Count is 17 and N is between 26 and 35, the Complex count is $3 \times 17 = 51$. If the Count is 24 and N is between 56 and 75, the Complex count is $24 + 24/4 = 30$. If the Count is –21 and N is between 106 and 155, the Complex count is $-21 - (-21/4)$, that is (about) –16.

To avoid divisions by 4 during play we may use the following approximate table:

0, 1, 2 divided by 4 = 0	11, 12, 13, 14 divided by 4 = 3
3, 4, 5, 6 divided by 4 = 1	15, 16, 17, 18 divided by 4 = 4
7, 8, 9, 10 divided by 4 = 2	19, 20, 21, 22 divided by 4 = 5

We leave the reader to complete this table for higher counts.

The player who learned to count but does not want to make the effort necessary for mastering the Tables 5-8 may just bet as recommended in this section (at this stage this should not be too difficult) and then use the *Basic strategy* for Drawing and Standing, Doubling down and Splitting. The method remains very powerful, especially in games played with multiple decks.

A pamphlet containing strategies with several parameters and more structured tables may be obtained directly from the authors (P.O. Box 8679, Chicago, Illinois, 60680).

4
BACCARAT

Baccarat is a card game* played at a table the layout of which, except for minor variations in the design, is shown in Fig. 1.

The players sit on chairs, behind the areas of the table marked by one of the numbers 1 to 12. The game is conducted by three Casino employees, who are positioned around the table as shown in Fig. 1.

Eight decks of cards, placed in a shoe (dealing box) are generally used. *Two hands* are dealt from the shoe, not by the dealers, but by one of the players. One of these hands is called the *Player's hand*, the other the *Banker's hand*. The players may wager on either of these two hands, or even on both if they wish. Bets are placed generally with currency or, sometimes, with large denomination chips. The players keep their currency and chips in front of them, in the areas marked by the numbers 1 to 12. The player who has the shoe is called the "Banker." Being the Banker presents neither advantage nor disadvantage for the player.

We shall explain below how the Player's and Banker's hands are dealt

---

*Baccarat is a game of European origin. Here we describe the variant played on the North American continent.

and completed, how the bets are placed and, once the hands are completed, which one wins.

In Baccarat the players gamble against the Casino. The House pays the winning bets and collects the losing ones.

Every Baccarat table has a *Minimum* and a *Maximum* bet limit. In plush Casinos, the *Minimum* bet limit is $5 or more often $20. The *Maximum* bet limit is $2,000. More recently, smaller Casinos have also introduced Baccarat. Lower bet limits are offered in these places.

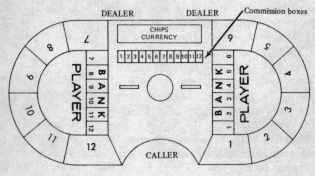

Fig. 1

The hands dealt in the game of Baccarat contain at least *two* and at most *three* cards. To describe the game it is necessary to explain what we mean by the value of such a hand. The values of Baccarat hands and Blackjack hands are defined differently.

THE VALUE OF A BACCARAT HAND

In Baccarat the tens and the face cards (Jacks, Queens and Kings) are counted 10.* The Aces are counted 1. All the

---

*Some authors count the tens and the face cards zero. Surprising as it may be, this does not change the values of Baccarat hands.

other cards are counted as their face values indicate. For instance

are counted 10, 2, 1 and 7 respectively.

The cards suits (clubs, diamonds, heart and spades) have no significance in Baccarat.

To obtain the value of a given hand we proceed as follows: First, we add the numbers corresponding to the cards in the hand. If the sum is a *one-digit* number then *the value of the hand is this sum.* If the sum is a *two-digit* number* *the value of the hand is the second digit.* For example, if the sum is the two-digit number 29, then the value of the hand is 9. If the sum is 17 the value of the hand is 7. If the sum is 10 the value of the hand is 0.

Here are several further examples. Consider the hands:

The sum of the numbers corresponding to the cards in the hand in Fig 2a is the one-digit number 5. Hence, the value of this hand is 5.

The sum of the numbers corresponding to the cards in the hand in Fig. 2b is the two-digit number 21. Since the second digit of 21 is 1, the value of the hand in Fig. 2b is 1.

The sum of the numbers corresponding to the cards in the hand in Fig. 2c is 30. Hence the value of this hand is 0.

The value of the hand in Fig. 2d is 7. The value of the hand in Fig. 2e is 1. The value of the hand in Fig. 2f is 2.

---

*The numbers 0, 1, 2, . . . , 9 are the *one-digit* numbers. The numbers 10, 11, . . . , 99 are the *two-digit* numbers. Therefore, there are ten one-digit numbers and 90 two-digit numbers.

Fig. 2a-f

Notice that the *lowest value* a Baccarat hand may have is 0. The highest value a hand may have is 9. A hand consisting of two cards and having a value of 8 or 9 is called a *natural*.

THE GAME

Baccarat is played with from 1 to 12 players (or even more, if the layout is so that more chairs can be accommodated).

The game proceeds as follows: Assume for example, that there are three players at the table, George, John and Sandi. Assume that George decides to wager on the Banker's hand

and that John and Sandi decide to wager on the Player's hand (see Fig. 3). We observe that *all* the players may wager on the Banker's hand or *all* the players may wager on the Player's hand, if they wish so.

George will place his bet in the *Bank box* 8. Sandi and John will place their bets in the areas marked X and Y respectively.

If Sandi had decided to wager on the Banker's hand instead of the Player's hand, then she would have placed her bet in the Bank box marked 3. In any case, the *position of the bets* will always show on which one of the two hands the respective players wagered.

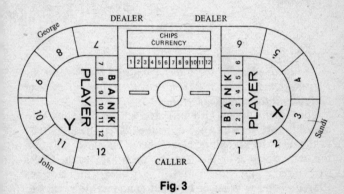

Fig. 3

Assume that George is given the shoe with cards. After all the bets are placed and *at the request of the Caller* (see Fig. 1), George will start dealing.* Successively he will give (slide) one card to the Caller, one card to himself, again one card to the Caller and finally one card to himself (see Fig. 4). All these cards are dealt face down.

---

*The player who is dealing (that is the Banker) is not required to wager on the Banker's hand. This player, however, must be active, that is, wager on one of the two Baccarat hands.

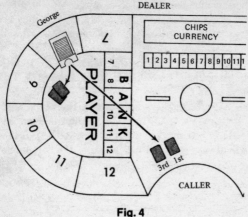

Fig. 4

The cards given to the Caller (first and third) form the Player's hand. The cards George dealt to himself (second and fourth) form the Banker's hand.

The Caller will now give the Player's hand (face down) to one of the players who wagered on the Player's hand, usually to the one who placed the highest bet. This player will turn the two cards face up and will give them back to the Caller (isn't this a silly little rule?). The Caller will place the Player's hand in front of him and announce its value (see Fig. 5). If everybody wagers on the Banker's hand, the Caller will turn the cards face up.

Now George (the Banker) will turn the Banker's hand face up and give it to the Caller. The Caller will again place the Banker's hand in front of him (but behind the Player's hand) and announce its value (see Fig. 5).

If *at least one* of the two hands has either the value 8 or the value 9, the two hands are compared and the one having the highest value *wins*. Of course, the hands may tie, that is, both may have the same value.

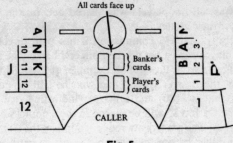

Fig. 5

When none of the initial two hands has the value of 8 or 9, *a third card may have to be dealt to one or to both hands*. The rules which stipulate whether or not third cards should be dealt will be fully explained further below, in the *Third card rule* section. Once the Player's and Banker's hands are completed (by dealing third cards if necessary) they are compared and the one having the highest value wins.

It may happen again that the two hands tie. When they do, nobody wins or loses. The players may remove or change their bets if they wish.

We observe that no matter how many players are at the table, only two hands are dealt. The players bet, at their choice, on one of these two hands.

THE SETTLEMENT

When the Player's hand wins, all the players who wager on this hand *win even money*. The players who wagered on the Banker's hand lose, and their bets are collected by the House.

When the Banker's hand wins all the players who wagered on this hand *win an amount equal to their bets minus a 5% commission*. For instance, if the Banker's hand has the highest value and George wagered $100 on this hand, he will win $95 (observe that 5% of $100 is $5). When the Banker's hand wins, all the players who placed bets on the Player's hand lose their money.

Generally, the 5% commission is not paid directly each time a player wins a bet on the Banker's hand. The adopted procedure is as follows: For example, if George wagered $100 on the Banker's hand and won he will be paid even money (that is $100) and a marker indicating that George owed the Casino $5 will be placed in the Commission box 8 (see Fig. 1). The players are requested to pay the (total) commission either before the next shuffle of the cards or when they leave the table.

No commission is removed from a win corresponding to a bet on the Player's hand or in case of a tie.

Once the settlement is made, the cards which were used are discarded in a box in the center of the table. If *enough* cards are left in the shoe, new hands are dealt. If not, the cards are shuffled and the game starts again.

The Banker (the player who deals) keeps the shoe as long as the Banker's hand does not lose. Once it loses, the shoe moves to the player on the right. Players do *not* have to accept the shoe and deal. When they do accept it, they may pass the shoe to their right any time a hand has been completed.

The fact that no commission is removed from the wins corresponding to bets on the Player's hand might appear to indicate that it is advantageous for the player to bet on this hand. However this is *not so*, since the Banker's hand wins more often. In fact, the player who places bets on the Banker's hand is somewhat better off than the player who places bets on the Player's hand, but the difference is very small.

Our calculation of percentages (without assuming "an infinite deck") gave results similar to those in Refs. 18 and 19. The House edge, as far as the Player's hand is concerned is somewhat more than 1.2%. The edge as far as the Banker's hand is concerned is about 1.1%.

THIRD CARD RULES

As we have said previously, if *at least one* of the initial (two-card) hands has a value of 8 or 9, then no further cards are dealt. The settlement is made immediately on the basis of the values of the hands.

However, if none of the initial hands has the value of 8 or 9, a third card may have to be dealt to one or both hands. The dealing of these cards is done according to rules which, for the general information of the reader, we explain below. The players do not really need to know these rules, since the Caller always instructs the Banker as to when to deal. In fact, it is important to remember *not* to deal unless the Caller instructs you to.

The Player's hand is acted upon first. There are two rules concerning this hand and they are as follows:*

The Player's hand draws** a third card when it has one of the values

0, 1, 2, 3, 4 or 5.

The Player's hand stands when it has one of the values

6 or 7.

The third card dealt to the Player's hand is placed as shown in Fig. 6. The third card dealt to the Banker's hand is placed in a similar way.

We observe that the above rules are independent of the Banker's hand. *Among the Third card rules concerning the Banker's hand the first two rules are independent of the Player's hand but the others are not.*

---

*From here on we assume that none of the two initial hands is a natural.

**To shorten certain phrases below we say that "the hand draws" or "the hand stands" instead of "a card is dealt to the hand" or "no cards are dealt to the hand." Further similar terminology will be used without explanation.

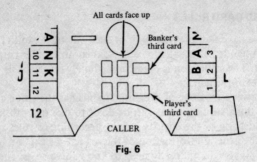

All cards face up

Banker's third card

Player's third card

CALLER

Fig. 6

The Banker's hand draws a third card when it has one of the values

0, 1 or 2.

The Banker's hand stands when it has the value

7.

When the Player's hand stands:

The Banker's hand draws a third card when it has one of the values

3, 4 or 5.

The Banker's hand stands when it has the value

6.

When the Player's hand draws:

With a value of 3 the Banker's hand draws a third card if the Player's hand has drawn a 0, 1, 2, 3, 4, 5, 6, 7 or 9 and stands otherwise. Hence the Banker's hand stands if the Player's hand drew an 8.

With a value of 4 the Banker's hand draws a third card if the Player's hand has drawn a 2, 3, 4, 5, 6 or 7 and stands otherwise.

With a value of 5 the Banker's hand draws a third card if

the Player's hand has drawn a 4, 5, 6 or 7 and stands otherwise.

With a value of 6 the Banker's hand draws a third card if the Player's hand has drawn a 6 or 7 and stands otherwise.

GENERAL REMARKS

Casino operators try to surround Baccarat with a special atmosphere. The area where the game is played is partitioned, although it is so placed that everybody can see what is going on inside, and the dealers conducting the game are generally in formal attire. An additional Casino supervisor sits "kingly" on a throne dominating the area. As a further attraction, relatively good-looking women (who are Casino employees) are always at the tables.

In a certain sense the Casinos are successful in their efforts to lure gamblers, especially large bettors, into playing this game. After all, percentagewise, Baccarat is one of the best games offered to the players. As we have seen the House edge is close to 1% and therefore only large, or very large bets, will bring enough profits.*

In Baccarat the players have no options as far as the play of hands is concerned. Thus Baccarat cannot be played "badly." Blackjack is of course a better game for the player than all other Casino games, but only when played skillfully. Baccarat is advertised as the best game for the player. This is certainly not true, even if we exclude Blackjack. Pass line bets and Don't pass line bets, with corresponding Odds, are better percentage bets for the player.

Some time ago Casinos offered certain additional "side bets." The players would wager that the Banker's hand would have the value 8, or that it would have the value 9 or that it would be a natural. E. O. Thorp, of Blackjack fame,

---

*We notice that 1% of $20 is more than 10% of $1.

and some of his associates, exploited the side bets in their favor by skillful play, and won a substantial amount. When the Casino operators realized what was happening the problem was simply and swiftly solved. The side bets were dropped. After all, only a few players understood these bets. Other types of side bets have been offered more recently. They will not be discussed here since they have not yet been standardized and do not offer any advantage for the players.

A game which might be of interest is Baccarat played with dice. The game could be played under rules similar to those we have explained in the previous sections, on a table with a simple layout. As far as this game is concerned, various types of side bets could be added without any *danger*.

Recently the game of Baccarat was offered at tables similar to those used for Blackjack, but of course with a different layout. Baccarat played in this manner seems to be attractive to very many players. Not only high-rollers, but also many low-rollers will now be able to enjoy the game.

5
SLOT MACHINES AND KENO

This chapter will be quite short, since there are only a few useful things to say concerning Slot machines and Keno.

Slot machines (or Slots) are found in many parts of the world. However, nowhere are they so numerous as in Nevada.

In Nevada, every Casino, plush or not, has a large variety of Slot machines. Such machines can be also found in airports, bus terminals, etc. This way departing tourists are given every opportunity to try their luck until the last moment.

Most Slot machines have three, four or more *vertical reels* (*wheels*) on which various symbols are marked. A place to insert your coins is provided and there is a relatively large handle on the right side of the machine.*

It is very easy to play the machines. Just insert your coins and pull the handle. The reels will start to move, and finally, after several rotations will stop. Whether or not you win depends on the *outcome*, that is on the symbols which appear on the *center line*. The *center line* is either indicated by an arrow or is drawn on a windshield covering part of the reels.

---

*This is one of the reasons why Slot machines got the appropriate name of "One arm bandits."

The payoff, in case of a win, also depends on these symbols. Winning combinations and their payoffs are posted on the machines.

Some outcomes, consisting usually of the *same* symbol on each one of the reels, are called *Jackpots*. The Jackpots give the player the largest wins. Additional premiums are sometimes given to the players who hit a Jackpot. Some Slot machines have only one Jackpot, others several.

For instance, in the case of certain three reelers the Jackpot consists of *three bars*. For one nickel such an outcome might pay $7.50. Some Slot machines offer much higher payoffs, for example $5,000 or even more, for $1. Of course the occurrence of such Jackpots is extremely improbable.

When you hit a Jackpot, bells might start ringing and/or lights might start flashing and everybody (?) is happy. Small wins will be paid automatically by the machine, but Jackpots are not necessarily paid in this way. Most machines pay only *part* of the win corresponding to a Jackpot. The rest is paid by an attendant. The attendant has to verify that the player has hit a Jackpot. If the machine is played again before this is done, the Jackpot *will not be paid*. Surprising as it may seem, many players do not realize that they hit a Jackpot, or do not notice that the machine did not pay fully the win.

If we knew how many symbols of each kind were marked on each reel and if we knew that the reels were not built (or set) in such a way that they stop more often in certain positions than in others, then it would be easy to compute the House take. Of course, we could determine a Slot machine take by gathering lengthy data. But there are so many types of such machines. In any case, based on the information we have we estimate the take of most Slot machines to be somewhere between 2.5% and 25%.

As we have already said, the winning outcomes and corresponding payoffs are clearly posted on each Slot machine. We consider that it will be only fair to request the Slot machine operators also to clearly post the machine's take. In fact this should be requested not only for Slot machines, but for all games where the outcome does not depend on the player's strategy.

Cigarette manufacturers are forced to post warning labels on their products. We observe that you smoke, if you do, of your own will and that nobody forces you to do so. If the House take would be posted this would serve only as fair information to the players. It would be nice to see warnings like this:

> The greatest machine on Earth.
> Pays four cents for every nickel.

After all losing money might be more unhealthy than smoking.

After the publication of the first edition of this volume, some of the Casinos started to post *Global* information concerning the take of some of their Slot machines.

Before concluding the first part of the chapter, we notice that most Slot machine players are women. Since women are now so liberated, we think that it is time that they liberate themselves from Slot machines also. After all, there are games much more favorable (for the player) and interesting and these games do not require brute force. For example Blackjack is such a game; and you can be assured that if you learn the Hit and Stand rules, you always split (A, A) and (8, 8), you always double down on hard 11 and double on hard 10 (when the dealer's up card is not a 10 or 11) you will be a much better player than most.

Keno is another game which at present is very much advertised in Nevada. Several years ago luxury Casinos would not even offer this game. But the situation has changed. You can now play the game in practically every Casino which is large enough.

Keno is in fact a lottery. In every Casino the center of activity surrounding the game is in the area where the *Keno lounge* is. It is here that *drawings* take place every several minutes.

The eighty numbers 1 *to* 80 are marked on eighty small balls, which are placed in a cage. *Twenty* of these balls are successively drawn. The corresponding numbers are called by a dealer and simultaneously lighted on several *Keno boards* located in the Casino (such boards are found even in some of the Casino restaurants). These twenty numbers are the *winning numbers*, or the *outcome* corresponding to the drawing. Each drawing has a specific number, usually referred to as *the game number*. The game number appears on the Keno boards before the corresponding drawing.

Assume now that Sandi decides to play Keno. She proceeds as follows: First she picks a blank Keno ticket, as the one in Fig.1. Such tickets are free and are easily found in the Keno lounge area, in the Casino restaurants, etc.

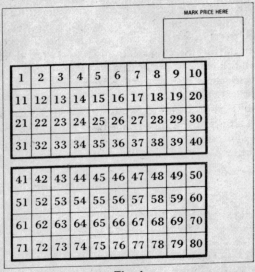

Fig. 1

She then selects from *one to fifteen numbers* and marks these numbers on the ticket as shown in Fig. 2. She also decides what she wants to wager and writes the amount of the bet on the right top corner of the ticket, as in Fig. 2.

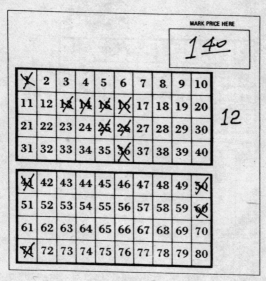

Fig. 2

We observe that Sandi selected the twelve numbers 1, 13, 14, 15, 16, 25, 26, 36, 41, 50, 60, 71 and that the amount of her bet is $1.40.*

The ticket is now ready. Sandi will take it to a *Keno writer* in the Keno lounge area, and will give him the amount of her bet (in this case $1.40) and the ticket. She will receive an *authorized* copy of the original one on which *the number of*

---

*The amount of the set is usually either a multiple of 70 cents (that is $0.70, $1.40, $2.10, $2.80, etc.) or a multiple of $1 (that is $1, $2, $3, $4, etc.).

the next drawing (or game) is printed on the right top corner, as shown in Fig. 3.*

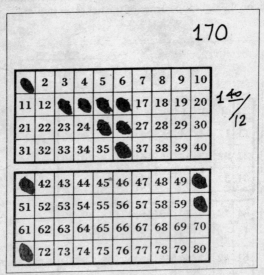

Fig. 3

Sandi will now wait (breathlessly!?) for the drawing number 170. If enough numbers on her ticket match those that appear on the board, she wins. If six numbers match, she will receive $6.00.** If seven numbers match she will receive $40.00. If all the numbers on Sandi's ticket are winning numbers she will be paid $25,000.

The number of matches required for a win and the corresponding payoffs depend on how *many* numbers you have selected and, of course, on the amount of your bet. All

---

*The ticket is good only for the drawing corresponding to the number marked on it.

**Small payoffs might differ from place to place.

the necessary information can be found in small booklets printed by the Casinos. These booklets are free and can be found near the same places where you found the Keno tickets.

Winning tickets must be collected immediately after the drawing. The tickets will *not* be paid if they are presented after the start of the next game.

We notice that the total payoff corresponding to a given drawing is $25,000 at most. This means that regardless how many winners there are, the Casino will not pay more than $25,000. Hence, in the extremely improbable situation, when the sum of the wins corresponding to a drawing exceeds $25,000, the winners will receive only part of the advertised payoffs.

Instead of bringing their tickets to a Keno writer, the players may give them to one of the many Keno girls found in the Casino and restaurants. These girls will bring you the authorized copy of your ticket and will also collect the winnings for you, if there are any. Since you will usually tip her, the price of your ticket will be indirectly increased when you ask the assistance of a Keno girl. Although these girls are Casino employees, the Casinos do not seem to assume responsibility if they somehow mishandle your tickets.

Under the present rules the House take in Keno is (with good approximation) 25% or more, depending on the type of ticket you write.

Is there any sense then in playing Keno? You should certainly not spend any substantial amount of money on this game. However, if you are ready to throw 70 cents or $1 away, and if you are close to a Keno lounge, you may instead play Keno. After all you may win $25,000 and then you can buy one or two mink coats or leave for a vacation in Rio de Janeiro.

The type of ticket described above is the most popular one, probably because it is the easiest to mark. There are however other types of tickets a player may write. For instance the

Way tickets, Combination tickets, $1 *Special tickets,* 12 *spots, High-low tickets,* etc. The Keno booklets, distributed by the Casinos, which we have mentioned above give further information about such tickets. As far as the House edge is concerned, these other types of tickets do not present *any* advantage for the player. Their only justification is that you may write "more tickets" faster. For general information we shall briefly describe two such tickets below:*

The ticket in Fig. 4, for example, is equivalent to *three tickets* marked as follows: On one of them the numbers in

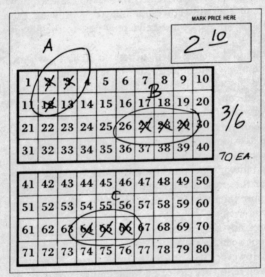

Fig. 4

groups A and B are selected. On the second one the numbers in groups A and C are selected. Finally, on the third, the

---

*The letters A, B, C, D do not appear on the tickets used in play.

numbers in the groups B and C are selected. The bet on each one of these tickets is $0.70.

The ticket in Fig. 5 is equivalent to 6 (= 1 + 1 + 4) tickets. On *two* of these tickets are marked the numbers in the groups

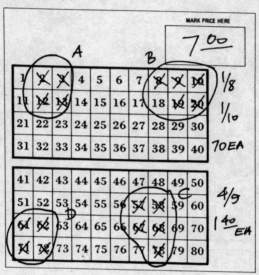

Fig. 5

A and D (eight numbers)

and

B and C (ten numbers),

respectively. The bet on each one of these two tickets is $0.70. On each one of the other four tickets *nine* numbers are marked. The marked numbers are respectively those in groups

A, B   A, C   D, B   D, C

The bet on each one of these four tickets is $1.40.

BIBLIOGRAPHY

1. "Argentina bank breakers," Time (February 12, 1957).
2. R. Baldwin, W. Cantey, H. Maisel and J. McDermott, *Playing Blackjack to Win. A New Strategy for the Game of 21*, M. Barrows & Co., Inc., New York, 1957.
3. J. R. Crawford, *How to Be a Consistent Winner in the Most Popular Card Games*, Doubleday and Co., Inc., New York, 1953.
4. R. A. Epstein, *The Theory of Gambling and Statistical Logic*, Academic Press, New York, 1977.
5. G. L. Fraikin, *Inside Nevada Gambling*, Exposition Press, New York, 1962.
6. B. Friedman, *Casino Games*, Golden Press, New York, 1973.
7. P. Griffin, *The rate of gain in player expectation for card games characterized by sampling without replacement and an evaluation of card counting systems*, (in Gambling and Society, Charles Thomas Publishing Co., Springfield, Illinois, 1975).
8. J. Kemeny and J. L. Snell, "Game-theoretic solution of Baccarat," *American Math. Monthly* (Aug.-Sept., 1957).
9. M. MacDougall, *MacDougall on Dice and Cards*, Coward-McCann, Inc., New York, 1944.
10. W. I. Nolan, *The Facts of Baccarat*, Gambler's Book Club, Las Vegas, 1970.
11. Ed Reid and O. Demaris, *The Green Felt Jungle*, Pocket Books Inc., New York, 1964.
12. L. Revere, *Playing Blackjack as a Business*, Lyle Stuart Inc., New York, 1973.
13. J. Scarne, *Scarne on Cards*, Crown Publishers Inc., New York, 1967 (see especially the part on cheating methods).
14. *Scientific American*, "How to beat the game" (April 1961).
15. E. O. Thorp, *Favorable Strategy for Twenty-one*, National Academy of Science, Proc. XLVII, 1961.
16. E. O. Thorp, *Beat the Dealer*, Random House, New York, 1966.
17. E. O. Thorp and W. Walden, *The fundamental theorem of card counting*, International J. of Game theory, 2, No. 2, 1973.
18. W. Walden, *Solution of games by computation*, Ph.D. thesis, New Mexico State U., 1964.
19. A. Wilson, *The Casino Gambler's Guide*, Harper and Row, New York, 1965.

APPENDIX

THE CONTENTS OF THIS APPEN-
DIX ARE COMPLETELY UNNEC-
ESSARY FOR READING AND MAS-
TERING THE PLAYING STRATE-
GIES DESCRIBED IN THIS VOL-
UME. THE APPENDIX IS IN-
CLUDED HERE FOR THE READER
WITH THEORETICAL INCLINA-
TIONS.

PROBABILITY

1. Basic Ideas

If an *urn* contains, for example 7
balls, all of them having the same
characteristics (that is size, weight,
etc.) and if we pick one of them
(without looking into the urn) then
each one of the seven balls is as likely
to be selected. We say that the *probability* that any particular ball in the
urn be selected is 1/7.

In general, when an element is
chosen from a *finite set* (or collection)
X, in such a way that every object is
equally likely to be selected, the probability $P(E)$ that the selected object is
from a *subset E* of X is given by

$$P(E) = \frac{\text{number of elements of } E}{\text{number of elements of } X}. \quad (1)$$

Otherwise said, the probability of the
event which consists of selecting a ball

from the subset E, an event which we shall denote again by the letter E, is given by Eq. (1).

The probability $P(E)$ measures in a certain sense the likelihood that E will occur. The larger $P(E)$ is, the more likely it is that the event E will occur. This is quite obvious if we notice that $P(E)$ increases when the number of elements in E increases and that the larger the number of elements of E is, the more likely it is that the chosen object be from E.

If the seven balls in the urn we have mentioned before have the same characteristics, except for the fact that *four* are green and *three* are red, then the probability that the selected ball is green is 4/7. In fact, in this case we may assume X to be the set of all balls in X and E the subset consisting of the green balls. Since X has 7 elements and E, 4 elements, Eq. (1) gives $P(E) = 4/7$.

Now we assume that we perform n successive selections from the urn (we place the ball back in the urn after each selection) and that k is the number of times the chosen ball was green. Hence, k is the number of times the event E consisting of ths selection of a green ball has occurred during the n trials. Then the fraction

$$\frac{k}{n}$$

is termed the *frequency* of the event E in our series of n trials. Of course we may introduce in the same way the frequency of other events of the same or more general type.

It is an extremely interesting experimental fact, and this is what makes the importance of *probability theory* in so many and varied applications, that *the larger the number n is, the more likely it is for k/n to be close to the probability of E*. Hence in a certain sense the frequency of the event approximates its probability.

In certain cases we may even deduce what the probability of an event is (or at least find an approximate value of its probability) by using its frequency. For instance assume again that we have an urn containing 7 balls, 4 green and 3 red, but that this time the balls are quite different. What is the probability that if we pick a ball from the urn, the selected one is green? Since we want the probability to indicate a practical measure of the chance of selecting a green ball, we cannot of course anymore say that it is 4/7. For example if the green balls are very large when compared with the red balls, it is likely that we shall be selecting always green balls. How do we estimate then the probability of the event E which consists of the selection of a green ball?

One method is to make a *long* series of selections, to count the number of times k the event E occurs and to use the frequency k/n as the probability of E. An even better method would be to make *several* series of selections and to take for probability the *average* of the corresponding frequencies.

We observe that the setting we have described at the beginning of the section is general and can be used for discussing many various problems. The selection of an object from a finite set X can also be performed in many ways. For example consider a roulette wheel. Let X be the set of the 38 symbols 0, 00, 1, 2, . . . , 36. We may decide to chose an object from X by the following method. We give the wheel a push in one direction and spin a ball in the opposite one. If the ball drops finally on 9, we say that 9 has been selected. It should be quite obvious that if the wheel is *honest* then the probability that any one of the objects of X is selected is 1/38.

We also notice here that in certain cases we may have to consider experiments leading to an infinity of events. The probability cannot be defined anymore by Eq. (1) in such situations (for instance we cannot perform the division in that formula). However the frequency of an event can still be defined and used to estimate its probability.

2. A Simple Example

Consider a usual deck consisting of 52 cards. If the deck is *honest* and you perform a *cut*, then each one of the 52 cards is equally likely to end as the top card. Hence the probability that any particular card becomes the top card after the cut is 1/52. Since the usual deck contains 4 Aces, the probability that an Ace becomes the top card is $4/52 = 1/13$. Since the deck contains 16 Tens (here we count the cards as in Blackjack) the probability that the top card after the cut is a Ten is $16/52 = 4/13$.

Assume that we play Blackjack, that the dealer's up card is an Ace and that we have received the usual 2 cards (we also assume that these are all the cards we have seen). What is the probability that the dealer has a Blackjack, once we see that his up card is an Ace? The answer is quite simple. If our hand does not contain any Tens, then the probability is

$$16/49 \quad \text{(or about 0.3265306)}$$

(since 49 cards remain in the deck and 16 of these are Tens). If our hand consists of 2 Tens then the probability that the dealer has a Blackjack is

$$14/49 \quad \text{(or about 0.2857143)}.$$

As we have already indicated in the chapter on Blackjack, if you see only the dealer's up card and your two cards then you should not take insurance. In any case the above remarks show that if you were to take insurance (which you definitely should not do in this case) it would be more advantageous to take it when your hand is for instance (4, 6) than when it is (10, 10). In fact, there is a better chance for the dealer to have a Blackjack when your hand is (4, 6), than when it is (10, 10). To decide when it is advantageous to take insurance you need an additional concept called Expectation. This will be discussed later.

We take this opportunity to observe that the usual

meaning given to the word insurance (i.e., to insure valuable things) has absolutely nothing to do with the corresponding bet in Blackjack. The bet could have been called *Shirley* as well. Of course at least some of the gambling house operators must have noticed that the use of the word *insurance* will cause a lot of players to insure when they should not, and hence substantially increase the take.

3. Certain Probabilities in Craps

In the game of Craps, on a Come-out roll, the player who places a Pass line bet wins if the outcome is 7 or 11 and loses if the outcome is 2, 3 or 12. If the outcome is any other number, for instance 8, that number becomes the *Point*. Then the dice continue to be thrown until either 7 or 8 is rolled. If 7 is rolled first, the Pass line bettors lose. If 8 is rolled first, the Pass line bettors win even money.

When you throw two dice, 36 *different outcomes are possible*. We understand this easily if we assume that one of the dice is white and the other is red. If for example 1 is rolled with the white dice and 3 with the red one, we say that the outcome is (1, 3). It is now obvious that the possible outcomes are

(1,6)	(2,6)	(3,6)	(4,6)	(5,6)	(6,6)
(1,5)	(2,5)	(3,5)	(4,5)	(5,5)	(6,5)
(1,4)	(2,4)	(3,4)	(4,4)	(5,4)	(6,4)
(1,3)	(2,3)	(3,3)	(4,3)	(5,3)	(6,3)
(1,2)	(2,2)	(3,2)	(4,2)	(5,2)	(6,2)
(1,1)	(2,1)	(3,1)	(4,1)	(5,1)	(6,1)

Table 1

Whence there are in all 36 possible outcomes and it is obvious that all these outcomes are equally possible.

As we have indicated in the chapter on Craps, we are often interested not directly in the pair of numbers we have rolled but in their sum. For instance if we have thrown (4, 6) we often say that we rolled 10. Inspecting Table 1 we see that 7 can be rolled in 6 ways, 11 in 2 ways, 2 in 1 way, 3 in 2 ways and 12 in 1 way. All the other outcomes will establish a Point on a Come-out roll. Since

$$6 + 2 + 1 + 2 + 1 = 12,$$

it follows that there are 36 – 12 = 24 ways to determine a Point. Hence the *probability of establishing a Point on a Come-out roll is*

$$\frac{24}{36} = \frac{2}{3}.$$

Hence on the average (or in the long run) 2 out of every 3 rolls will establish a Point.

Once the Point has been established the dice are rolled until either 7 or the Point is thrown. The following list of probabilities is therefore of interest (here for any two numbers a, b we denote $P(a, b)$ the probability that a is rolled before b):

$P(6, 7) = P(8, 7) = 5/11$ $P(7, 6) = P(7, 8) = 6/11$
$P(4, 7) = P(10, 7) = 3/9$ $P(7, 4) = P(7, 10) = 6/9$
$P(5, 7) = P(9, 7) = 4/10$ $P(7, 5) = P(7, 9) = 6/10$

Table 2

The computation of the probabilities in Table 2 is relatively more difficult than that of the other probabilities already mentioned here. In fact, if we were to construct a formal mathematical model following the development of the game, and use in detail this model for our computations, we would have in particular to make use of infinite products of probability spaces. Of course we do not intend here to go as far. In any case, in the next paragraph we shall give an idea of the method of computation of $P(a, b)$.

4. The Computation of the Probabilities *P(a, b)*

We shall discuss the computation of one of these probabilities, for instance $P(6, 7)$.

We notice before proceeding further than an inspection of Table 1 shows that the probability of rolling 6 *in one given throw* of two dice is 5/36 and that of rolling neither 6 nor 7 *in one given throw* is 25/36.

Assume now that we start throwing successively two dice. Then the event $A(6, 7)$, which consists in rolling 6 before 7, will occur if and only if *one* of the events we list below occurs:

Event A_1, consisting of rolling 6 on the first throw; *Event A_2*, consisting of rolling neither 6 nor 7 on the first throw, but rolling 6 on the second throw; *Event A_3*, consisting in rolling neither 6 nor 7 on the first two throws, but rolling 6 on the third roll; in general the *Event A_n*, consisting in rolling neither 6 nor 7 on the first $n - 1$ throws, but rolling 6 on the nth throw.

Since no two of the events $A_1, A_2, A_3, \ldots, A_n, \ldots$ may both occur (these events are *incompatible* during the same sequence of throws) a general property in probability theory tells us that the probability of $A(6, 7)$ (which we have noted $P(6, 7)$) is the sum of the probabilities $P(A_1)$, $P(A_2)$, $P(A_3)$, $\ldots, P(A_n), \ldots$ of the events $A_1, A_2, A_3, \ldots, A_n \ldots$ Hence

$$P(6, 7) = P(A_1) + P(A_2) + P(A_3) + \ldots + P(A_n) + \ldots \quad (2)$$

Now $P(A_1) = 5/36$. To compute $P(A_2)$ we observe that A_2 occurs if and only if both of the following events occur: neither 6 nor 7 is rolled on the first throw (first event) and 6 is rolled on the second throw (second event). Since the probabilities of these two events are 25/36 and 5/36 respectively, and since these two events are *independent* (the outcome of one of them does not influence the outcome of the other in any way) we deduce from probability theory that

$$P(A_2) = (25/36) (5/36).$$

In the same way we obtain that

$$P(A_3) = (25/36)^2(5/36)$$

and in general

$$P(A_n) = (25/36)^{n-1}(5/36)$$

for every n. It follows that

$$P(6,7) = (5/36) + (25/36)(5/36) + (25/36)^2(5/36) + \ldots$$
$$+ (26/36)^{n-1}(5/36) + \ldots$$
$$= (5/36)(1 + (25/36) + (25/36)^2 + \ldots + (25/36)^{n-1} + \ldots)$$
$$= (5/36)(1/(1 - (25/36))) = (5/36)(36/(36 - 25)) = 5/11.$$

By the same method we compute the other probabilities in the first column of the Table 2. To compute the probabilities in the second column is easy, once those in the first column have been computed. In fact, let $A(7, 6)$ be the event which consists in rolling 7 before 6. Since $A(6, 7)$ and $A(7,6)$ cannot occur at the same time (hence $A(6,7)$ and $A(7,6)$ are incompatible) and since one of these events must occur in our series of throws, a general property of probability tells us that the sum of the probabilities of $A(6, 7)$ and $A(7, 6)$ is 1 (in fact the property we use here is essentially the same we used to write Eq. (2)). Since $P(6, 7) = 5/11$ we deduce that $P(7, 6) = 1 - P(6, 7) = 1 - 5/11 = 6/11$.

EXPECTATION

1. Basic Ideas

Consider an urn containing a certain number of balls, part of them green and the others red. Assume that the probability of selecting a green ball from the urn is p and that of selecting a red ball is q. Since the two considered events are obviously incompatible and since one must occur, general properties of probability will imply $p + q = 1$.

Assume now that a Casino offers the following *game*: If the ball selected from the urn is green, we are paid \$5. If the ball selected is red we have to pay \$3. By definition then, the *Mathematical expectation* or simply the *Expectation* of the game is

$$E = 5p + (-3)q. \tag{3}$$

Now let us analyse this definition and see what is its practical meaning. Assume that

$$p = 4/7 \quad \text{and} \quad q = 3/7.$$

Then

$$E = 5(4/7) + (-3)(3/7) = (20-9)/7 = 11/7.$$

Since the probability of selecting a green ball is 4/7, it follows that in the long run, 4 times out of every 7 trials (games) we shall select a green ball. Hence in every 7 games we shall be paid 4 times \$5, that is \$20. In the same way we see that in every 7 games we shall have to pay 3 times \$3, that is \$9. Hence in every seven such games we make $20 - 9 = 11$ dollars. Hence *in the long run we make 11/7 dollars per game*. Notice that this is the value of the Expectation E.

To participate in a series of 7 games we need a capital of 7 times \$3, that is a capital of \$21. In fact it is possible that in one given series of 7 games (not in the long run) each time a red ball is selected. Then we shall have to pay \$21 (if we do not pay the \$21 who knows what might happen!). We deduce that a capital of \$21 brings \$11. Hence a capital of \$3 brings \$11/7 (per game). Hence \$1 brings \$11/21 and hence \$100 will bring \$1100/21. Since

$$1100/21 = (\text{about}) \ 52.38095$$

it follows that this game will bring the player a profit of 52.38095%. What a nice game and what a nice Casino!

If the Casino pays \$7/4 when a green ball is selected and you pay \$7/3 when a red ball is selected, then

$$E = (7/4)(4/7) + (-7/3)(3/7) = 1 + (-1) = 0.$$

In this case reasoning as above we see that \$100 brings \$0, hence in this game you have a profit of 0%.

Now assume that more realistically, the Casino pays \$0.50 when a green ball is selected and that you the player pay \$2 if a red ball is selected. Then

$$E = (1/2)(4/7) + (-2)(3/7) = -8/14.$$

Reasoning as in the first situation we see that this means that you the player will have to pay \$8/14 per game. Since you need a capital of \$2 to participate in each game, it follows that you lose \$8/28 per each dollar, or \$800/28 per each \$100 you "invest" in this game. Since

$$800/28 = (about)\ 28.571428$$

it follows that in this game you will lose 28.571428% of the money you risk. Hence if you play this game 500 times you will lose about \$285. If you get stubborn and play this game 5000 times you will certainly lose (there is no doubt about this) about \$2857.

Observe in conclusion, that the Expectation E, multiplied by 100 and divided by the amount you have risked per game (in the first situation this amount was \$3) gives *the percent advantage or disadvantage*. If $E > 0$ you have advantage, if $E < 0$ the Casino has advantage.

Of course we can define the Expectation for more general games. One such type of game is the following: Let A_1, A_2, . . . , A_n be n incompatible events which may occur as a result of a certain experiment. Assume also that one of the n events must occur. Let p_1, p_2, . . . , p_n be the corresponding probabilities of A_1, A_2, . . . , A_n. If we are paid \$$x_i$ when A_i (i

$= 1, 2, \ldots, n$) occurs, then the Expectation of the game is

$$E = p_1 x_1 + p_2 x_2 + \ldots + p_n x_n.$$

Here x_i might be ≥ 0 or ≤ 0 (3 is ≥ 0 and -3 is ≤ 0). If, say, x_2 is < 0, this would mean of course that you pay $\$x_2$ when A_2 occurs. Again the player has advantage if $E > 0$ and disadvantage if $E < 0$.

2. Insurance

Let X be a set of usual playing cards and assume that X contains at least one Ace. Denote by A the set of all Tens (counted as in Blackjack) in X. Denote by $n(A)$ and $n(X)$ the number of elements of A and X respectively.

Assume that a dealer deals himself two cards, one face up, one face down, and assume that the card face up is an Ace.

Clearly if p is the probability that the dealer has a Blackjack and q is the probability that he does not, then

$$p = \frac{n(A)}{n(X) - 1} \quad \text{and} \quad q = \frac{(n(X) - 1) - n(A)}{n(X) - 1}$$

Assume now that a player participates in a game played as follows: If the dealer has Blackjack the player will be paid $\$2$. If the dealer does not have Blackjack, the player will pay (lose) $\$1$. The Expectation corresponding to this game is

$$E = 2p + (-1)q = 2\,\frac{n(A)}{n(X) - 1} - \frac{(n(X) - 1) - n(A)}{n(X) - 1}$$

$$= \frac{2n(A) - (n(X) - 1) + n(A)}{n(X) - 1} = \frac{3n(A)}{n(X) - 1} - 1.$$

We deduce that $E > 0$ if and only if $n(A)/(n(X) - 1) > 1/3$, that is if and only if the number of Tens divided by the number of remaining cards is $> 1/3$. It is obvious that this shows that in an actual Blackjack game it is advantageous to insure if and only if the number of Tens divided by the number of remaining cards is > 1/3. To insure in the case when this fraction is just 1/3 will make no difference in the long run, except for decreasing the fluctuations in the player's capital. We may then conclude by saying that the player should insure only when the number of remaining Tens over the number of remaining cards is greater than or equal to 1/3.

As we have already said, if you do not keep track of the cards you should not insure. If you keep track of cards through certain Point counts, then certain relations which can be established between the number of the remaining Tens and these Point counts give us information which we can use to insure properly. When to insure when the player uses the Simple point count or the Complex point count, was indicated in the chapter on Blackjack.

Without presenting the corresponding computations, we want to say that the player who plays two hands, does not keep track of cards and insures* when the two hands held contain three Tens, loses in the long run about 17% of the amount of the insurance bets. It would be even worse to insure when the two hands were (10, 10) and (10, 10).

3. The Casino Advantage in the Case of the Big 6 Bet

Recall that when you place a bet on Big 6 you win even money if you roll 6 before 7 and lose your bet if 7 is rolled before 6.

The probability of rolling 6 before 7 is $P(6, 7) = 5/11$; that of rolling 7 before 6 is $P(7, 6) = 6/11$. Hence the Expectation corresponding to placing bets on Big 6 is

$$E = 1 \cdot (5/11) + (-1) \cdot (6/11) = -1/11$$
$$= \text{(about)} -0.0909090.$$

It follows that the player's disadvantage is about 9%.

---

*(In one-deck games, on the first round of play).

4. An Example of a Game of Strategy.

George and John are waiting in Las Vegas for a delayed plane for Chicago. To kill time John proposes to George to play the following game: We show simultaneously (no cheating!?!) either *one* or *two* fingers. When we show the same number of fingers, you (George) pay me $2. When I show one finger and you show two, I will pay you $1. When I show two fingers and you show one, I will pay you $3. Bored by the delay, and since at first the game appears to be even, George is ready to accept. However, after a few moments of thought he declines to play. Why?

The fact is that John can play in such a way that the game is favorable to him, *no matter* what George does. To see this let us first describe the situation by the following obvious diagram shown in Fig. 1.

$$\begin{array}{c} \text{George} \\ \begin{array}{cc} 1 & 2 \end{array} \\ \text{John} \begin{array}{c} 1 \\ 2 \end{array} \left(\begin{array}{cc} 2 & -1 \\ -3 & 2 \end{array} \right) \end{array}$$

Fig. 1

There are in all four possible events which we denote (1, 1), (1,2), (2,1) and (2,2). Here (1,1) is the event which consists of both players showing one finger, (1,2) the event which consists of John showing one finger and George two, etc.

Assume that John proceeds as follows: He shows *one finger* with probability* 5/8, and hence (since he must show

---

*This means that on the average John shows one finger five times on every eight games. We do not need much ingenuity to see how this can be done.

In Game — theoretic terminology we may say that John uses *the strategy* (5/8, 3/8).

either one or two fingers) *two fingers* with probability 3/8 ($=1$-5/8). Then John will be certain winner, *no matter* what George does.

In fact, assume that George shows *one finger* with probability p and *two fingers* with probability 9 ($p + q = 1$). Then the probabilities of the events

$$(1,1), (1,2), (2,1), (2,2)$$

are respectively.

$$(5/8)p, (5/8)q, (3/8)p, (3/8)q.$$

If $(1,1)$ or $(2,2)$ occurs, George loses (each time) \$2. If $(1,2)$ occurs, George gains \$1 and if $(2,1)$ occurs, George gains \$3. Hence the *Expectation* of this game (for George) is

$$E = (-2)(5/8)p + 1(5/8)q + 3(3/8)p + (-2)(3/8)q.$$

A simple computation leads to

$$E = (-1/8)p + (-1/8)q = (-1/8)(p+q) = -1/8$$

Hence *George will lose, in the long run, one eighth of a dollar per game*. If the plane is delayed for two hours and if George is stuborn, John will certainly win substantially more than the first class fare to Chicago.

If John does not realize that he should use the strategy (5/8, 3/8), the situation may change. For instance, if John uses the strategy (1/2, 1/2) and George uses the strategy (2/3, 1/3), then George will be a winner in the long run. The fact remains however that the game is so set, that if John constantly uses the strategy (5/8, 3/8) then he will be a certain winner, no matter what strategy George uses.

We introduced this example here since it shows again the interest of the *mathematical expectation* and also since it belongs to a branch of science known as Game theory, a branch that has numerous and varied applications in the analysis of conflicts among people or groups of people and hence in economics, military decisions, etc.

INDEX